Awesome

Hands-on

Activities
for Teaching

Literary Elements

By Susan Van Zile

SCHOLASTIC
PROFESSIONAL BOOKS

New York ■ Toronto ■ London ■ Auckland ■ Sydney
Mexico City ■ New Delhi ■ Hong Kong

Acknowledgments

This book is dedicated to the Giver and to the gifts in each of us that come through us but are not of us.

To my magnificent students who inspire me, teach me, and bring me great joy. I thank each of you for sharing your talents.

To my dear friend and co-teacher, Tammy Novick, for her invaluable support, insights, ideas, and encouragement.

To my colleagues for their inspiration, especially Sharon Cyron for her art work, collaboration, and generous spirit; Suzanne Shuey for her brilliance and talent, and my team for putting up with my antics.

To my maestro Phil Matthews who nurtures, develops, and celebrates creativity and humanity.

To Virginia Dooley, Editorial Director of Scholastic Grades 4–8 Professional Books, and Terry Cooper, Editor-in-Chief of Scholastic Professional Books, for giving me the courage and opportunity to live a dream.

To the Cumberland Valley School District for fostering professional development and growth.

To my friends and family for their love and enthusiasm.

To my husband Phil for being there and for his abiding love.

To my daughter Caroline for her artistic soul.

To my son Taylor for making me laugh and for his caring and understanding.

And to all the people at Scholastic who help each of us make a difference every day.

Table of Contents

Introduction

Rationale

Students are better able to understand and interpret novels, short stories, folk tales, and myths if they understand how the author organizes or structures the text. As different as these genres are, all of them share a common narrative structure. There are five basic components of narrative text (Pennsylvania Department of Education 1998):

1. Setting
2. Characters
3. Plot
4. Theme
5. Vocabulary

Teaching students these fundamental components is essential, because "when readers know how to utilize the structure of text to identify the information necessary for constructing meaning, their comprehension will improve" (Moore et al. 1989).

A second reason for providing instruction in the elements that comprise narrative text is that as the brain acquires new information, it creates patterns to make a meaningful context for learning material (Jensen 1998). The implication for teachers is that we enhance students' ability to comprehend text by teaching its inherent structure or pattern of organization. Jensen suggests that educators "simply read to kids and ask for patterns of organization."

Third, the activities included here are linked to both national and state standards. The National Standards for the English Language Arts (NCTE and IRA 1996) specify that students need to "apply a wide range of strategies to comprehend, interpret, evaluate, and appreciate texts." Learning about story elements that create narrative text structure is one strategy students need to construct meaning from the text. In addition, many states have developed specific standards for reading, analyzing, and interpreting literature, which include identifying, comparing, and evaluating literary elements.

A fourth reason to engage in activities designed to teach literary elements is that they help students develop an understanding of and appreciation for literature. Interacting with the text through a variety of hands-on activities motivates students and makes the literature come alive. Furthermore, as Tomlinson and Kalebfleisch (1998) note, the brain learns best when it "does" rather than "absorbs." Therefore, it is paramount to create meaningful activities that actively involve our students in the learning process.

Finally, because all students learn information in different ways, structuring activities that include visual, auditory, and tactile-kinesthetic components "can increase academic achievement and improve attitudes toward learning" (Green 1999). Most of the activities in this book are designed to address visual, auditory, and tactile-kinesthetic learners. In addition, numerous activities consider the eight intelligences defined by Howard Gardner. As Green suggests, "each person is unique in his [or her] particular combination of intelligences." Consequently, educators need to create learning experiences that give students opportunities to "exercise in their intellectual area of expertise."

Overview

This book includes a variety of activities teachers can use to teach four of the five components of narrative text: setting, character, plot, and theme. In addition, educators will find multiple intelligences activities designed to help students analyze various literary elements in a story or a novel. For example, as students create a physical game, they incorporate characters, setting, conflict, plot, and theme within it. Activities involving all of the elements of literature should be used when students are ready to proceed independently in their analysis of a story.

The activities here can be used with novels, short stories, folk tales, fairy tales, or myths. Because I use literature discussion groups and reader response journals in conjunction with these hands-on literary element activities, many of them are created for "home-based" cooperative groups of four. The criteria I use to form mixed, balanced groups are academic ability, gender, ethnicity, current social skills, and learning styles. Since I frequently work with cooperative groups, I have included direction sheets that designate specific group roles for the individual group members. These sheets are also structured to provide individual accountability. Students refer to the direction sheet to complete the activity independently. Where appropriate, I also include rubrics to evaluate the projects. The activities call for a variety of materials. Parents and our PTO (Parent Teacher Organization) provide many of my supplies. Often businesses in your community will make donations of supplies.

Although many of the activities are designed for cooperative groups, they can be adapted for individual use. Some of the activities, such as categorize a conflict, work best with partners. Others, such as the setting murals, are whole-class activities. For each activity, the purpose, the objective(s), the time allotment, materials needed, and step-by-step directions are included. If possible, student examples of the projects are included as well.

Most of these activities are designed to be used during or after reading and are part of guided and independent practice. To be truly effective, the activities here should be integrated with reader response journals and literature discussion groups so students have multiple ways of interacting with and interpreting text. To become proficient in their use of language, students need integrated experiences in reading, writing, speaking, and listening.

I hope that you and your students will enjoy trying these activities. Since I started using a hands-on approach to language arts, my classroom has changed dramatically. Instead of students sitting and passively absorbing information, they now are learning by doing. When I hear them say, "Great! It's time for English class. I can't wait to find out what we will do today," I know that what I am doing is working.

CHAPTER I

Setting

The Purpose of the Setting Activities

Mentally visualizing characters and events described in a story is one strategy employed by good readers. Research has found that using mental imagery leads to increased comprehension (Moore et al. 1989).

Since the setting can influence the plot, help create the mood, and affect what happens to the characters, being able to "see" the setting is important. Training students to form mental images can "enhance learning and increase retention" (Sousa 1995). The activities in Chapter 1 capitalize on the process of visualization and move students beyond talking about their mental images to actually creating them.

An Introduction to Setting

Provide students with a variety of photographs and/or postcards of intriguing places. Distribute one picture to each student. Ask students to write a brief description of the pictured setting using rich sensory language. Tell them that, since setting is both time and place, they should include a reference to time in their descriptions, such as the time of day, season of the year, or historical event. When they are finished, divide the class into small groups. Have group members place their cards facedown in a pile. One student shuffles the pile and turns the cards picture side up. Each student takes a turn reading aloud his or her description, and the group guesses which picture matches the description. As a class, discuss how the photographers created a mood for the setting. Then discuss how an author creates setting and mood in a story.

TEACHER TIP

Students often remember setting as where the story takes place. They forget that setting is both time and place. To reinforce this concept, I use movement or the bodily-kinesthetic intelligence. I have students say, "Setting is both time and place." When they say the word *time*, they point to a watch (it may be real or imaginary) on their wrist. When they say *place*, they use their hands to form the shape of a house. The thumbs and pinkies form the foundation; the tips of the index, middle, and ring fingers meet to form a triangle, which represents the roof.

ACTIVITY I

Setting Pop-ups

HOW TO USE THIS ACTIVITY: Individuals or cooperative groups can create the setting pop-ups. You can use this activity when literature groups are reading different books or stories. This way each group can share its pop-ups with the whole class to compare and contrast the settings.

If students are reading the same book or story, assign individuals or groups passages that describe different aspects of the setting so that students can discuss why the various settings are important and how the setting affects the plot. Discuss the moods created by the settings and connect them to the author's purpose.

OBJECTIVE: To create a pop-up page that depicts the setting in a novel

TIME: Two or three 40-minute class periods, or assign as homework

MATERIALS

Setting Pop-up Directions and Setting Pop-up Rubric (pages 19–22) • index cards • 9" x 12" pieces of oak tag (or Bristol board) • construction paper • markers, crayons, colored pencils • glue sticks • rulers • scissors • stickers (optional) • tissue paper (optional) • different-colored rolls of cellophane gift wrap

STEP-BY-STEP

1. Distribute a copy of the Pop-up Directions reproducible to each group of students. Instruct them to follow the directions and check off each one as they complete it. Review the Group Roles with students. You may want to help students find setting passages in their novels.

2. Have students draw a quick sketch of the setting and use the sketch to help plan the pop-up.

3. Before distributing the materials for constructing the pop-ups, model the process of folding the paper and cutting the tabs. Remind students to use a ruler to draw the tabs on which they glue the object that "pops out." The tabs should be at least 1" long but no longer than 1 1/2". The tabs should be between 1/2" and 1" wide. (See illustrations below.) If possible, show examples of finished products.

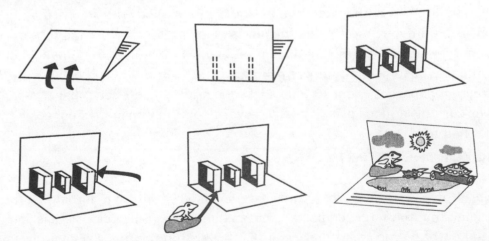

If students want to use a different color paper for the background, remind them to glue that paper onto the oak tag *before* they cut the tabs. Tell them to cut the tabs on the vertical lines only.

4. Brainstorm with students ways to make various pop-up pieces for their scenes.
5. Have students share the pop-ups in small groups or as a class.
6. Help students compare and contrast the various settings or interpretations of settings.
7. Use the Setting Pop-up Rubric for students to evaluate their own work and for you to evaluate their work.

TEACHER TIP

Ask students who have experience making pop-ups to show the class more complicated techniques. Provide how-to pop-up books for students to examine.

ACTIVITY 2

Setting Watercolors

A Verbal and Visual Project

Woods
Magical, mysterious
Terrifying, intriguing, tantalizing
Hub of the wheel
Forest

HOW TO USE THIS ACTIVITY: This activity may be used with any story or novel. I've used it with great success with *Tuck Everlasting*. In addition to creating a visual representation of the setting, students write cinquains describing the setting they paint.

OBJECTIVE: To create a visual and verbal representation of the setting through watercolor and poetry

TIME: Three to six 40-minute class periods

MATERIALS

copies of Setting Cinquain and Watercolor Rubric (page 23) • three buckets (two empty and one filled with water) and plastic pitchers filled with water (if a sink is not available in your room) • plastic bowls (such as large margarine tubs or whipped cream containers) • paintbrushes • Styrofoam meat trays • watercolor paints • Mongol pencils • pastels, white crayons • white tempera paint • 9" x 12" white drawing paper • 15" x 12" black construction paper for frames • glue sticks • masking tape • scrap paper • paper grocery bags • shower curtains and/or plastic bags to cover floor • newspaper • sponges • hair dryers (optional, but helpful)

PREPARING FOR THE ACTIVITY

Day 1

On an overhead projector, show an art transparency of a beautiful yet forbidding forest. Have students imagine that the forest contains a magical, mysterious secret. Then ask students to write a journal entry telling about the secret that lies within the forest. Encourage students to include the thoughts and feelings they experience as they imagine the forest.

Have partners share their journal entries. As a class, discuss the tone and mood of the

ART/LANGUAGE ARTS INTEGRATION

This project is a collaboration between the art and language arts departments. Suzanne Shuey, our art instructor, teaches the watercolor segment of the lesson, and I conduct the language arts portion.

One week before starting the project, Mrs. Shuey and I offer a two-day after-school workshop from 3:00 P.M. to 4:30 P.M. The purpose of this workshop is to demonstrate effective techniques for producing a watercolor painting. The students who attend the workshop become the "class experts" and help teach these techniques to their classmates.

painting and the techniques the artist used to create the mood. Then tell the class that, like an artist, an author paints a picture of the setting and the mood with words.

On the board, list the pages that describe various settings in the novel you are studying. Ask students to choose one of the settings listed and search the text for key words and phrases that describe the setting and mood. As they examine the text, they should write key words and phrases on index cards.

Next, have students form small groups based on the passages they selected. Have group members share the words and phrases on their index cards. They should also discuss their visual interpretation of the setting. After the small group discussions, meet as a whole class to discuss the importance various settings play in the novel.

Show students examples of landscape paintings. You can borrow these from the art teacher or use calendars or fine art books. Point out examples of background, foreground, middle ground, and perspective. For homework, distribute the drawing paper to students and ask them to complete a detailed sketch of the setting their group discussed.

Day 2

Before class starts, prepare the room for painting. You may want to place plastic shower curtains and/or plastic garbage bags over the floor and arrange desks into groups of four. Each group of four receives newspaper to cover the desks, one bowl of water, four paintbrushes, one set of watercolor paints, one pack of Mongol watercolor pencils, four meat trays, paper towels, and a paper grocery bag to use for trash.

If you do not have a sink in your room, fill plastic pitchers with water. These can be used to refill the plastic bowls. Post "Rules for Painting and Cleanup" on the board and provide a copy of the rules for each group.

When class begins, have students examine their sketches to be sure they have background, middle ground, and foreground. Provide students with informal feedback regarding their sketches. Show students the two basic principles of making an effective watercolor: creating a wash and adding details to the painting (directions for doing this are outlined below in Lessons 1 and 2). Be sure to have one dry, completed wash so that you can effectively demonstrate how to add details. As part of the lesson on adding detail, you may want to show students examples of various paintings, pointing out the techniques the artists used.

RULES FOR PAINTING AND CLEANUP

1. Fill water containers half full.
2. Use the pitchers to pour clean water.
3. Dump dirty water into the designated bucket or sink.
4. Use paper towels to clean out "contaminated" watercolors (colors are contaminated when the base color has other colors mixed in with it).
5. Rinse and dry the trays used for the washes.
6. Use a sponge and water to clean the desks.
7. Clean the brushes with water.

The demonstration takes 15 to 20 minutes. In the time remaining, students paint the washes onto the white construction paper. Creating the paintings takes three to four days. Students may need an extra day to add detail. The finished products are well worth the time students put into them. Seeing the watercolors hanging around the room makes students feel they are living in the book.

Getting Started and Making a Wash

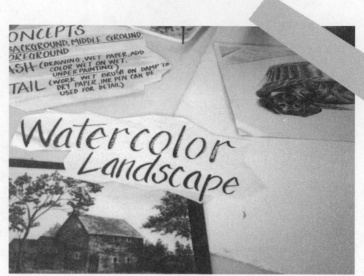

STEP-BY-STEP

1. Have each student draw a detailed sketch of the setting on white construction paper. Remind students to include foreground, middle ground, and background.

2. Tell students to tape their sketches to the desk.

3. Explain that areas marked with white crayon will resist the paint. If students are using the outlines technique (described on page 11), they should outline objects in their sketches before they paint.

4. Tell students to decide what colors to use for the wash. Encourage them to use different colors for different backgrounds. They should mix their colors in the tray and apply the wash to scrap paper to test.

5. Have students use a wet paper towel or a damp sponge to wet the sketch, section by section. Tell them to work from top to bottom, applying the wash with the paintbrush immediately after wetting a section.

6. Let the wash dry. To speed up this process, use a hair dryer.

7. Cleanup. Remind students to follow the Rules for Painting and Cleanup (see page 9).

LESSON 2

Add Details to Your Painting

Encourage students to try different techniques to add details to their paintings.

Technique 1: Dry Brush

a. Be sure that the paint on the construction paper is completely dry.

b. Remove excess water from the paint palette.

c. Dip the tip of the brush in water and then in concentrated pigment.

d. Use the tip of the brush to add detail to the painting.

Technique 2: Mongol Pencils

a. Hold the sharpened pencil sideways.

b. Use it to fill in the desired area.

c. Go over this area with a wet paintbrush.

Technique 3: Pastels

a. Be sure the painting is completely dry.

b. Apply pastels over the paint, and blend.

c. Cover the painting with a sheet of white copy paper to prevent smearing.

Technique 4: Outlines

a. Use white crayon to outline objects. Apply the white crayon before you paint.

b. Be sure the painting is dry. Use white tempera paint or black ink to outline objects.

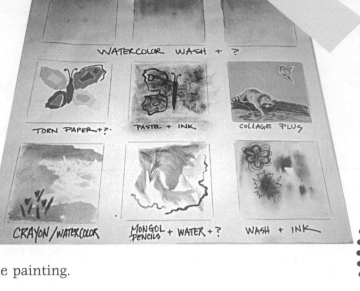

LESSON 3

Framing the Painting

STEP-BY-STEP

1. When the paintings are completely dry, have students place them facedown on the desk. Tell them to apply glue stick around the edges of the paper.

2. Then they use the glue stick to make a large *X* in the center of the paper.

3. Tell them to place the painting in the center of a sheet of black construction paper and smooth it down. Their paintings are now complete!

WRITING THE CINQUAINS

Review the settings portrayed in students' paintings. Explain that they will now write cinquains that describe the same setting.

How to Write a Setting Cinquain
Use the following pattern.

Noun

Adjective, adjective

Verb + ing, verb + ing, verb + ing

Four-word free statement

Synonym or equivalent for the topic

Example of a setting cinquain:

Woods

Magical, mysterious

Terrifying, intriguing, tantalizing

Hub of the wheel

Forest

To assist students who have difficulty writing, provide this simple form:

Setting Cinquain

_____
Noun

_____, _____
Adjective   adjective

_____, _____, _____
Verb + ing   verb + ing   verb + ing

_____ _____ _____ _____
Four-word statement

_____
Synonym

NOTE: Use the Setting Cinquain and Watercolor Rubric (page 22) to evaluate students' work.

After printing the cinquains from the computer, create an art and poetry gallery. Hang the poems and paintings throughout the classroom and hallway. Students tour the "art gallery" prior to discussing why the setting is important in a story.

> ## TEACHER TIP
> If you want to shorten the time for this activity, use Mongol pencils instead of watercolors. Assign the cinquains for homework.

Setting Postcards

HOW TO USE THIS ACTIVITY: To show students what might have happened when Mt. Vesuvius exploded, I use powerful visuals and a simple but effective hands-on experiment. Then in response to our introductory activities, the story, and discussions, students create a setting postcard that visually depicts the setting and verbally expresses the feelings and emotions of a visitor touring Pompeii the day Vesuvius erupted.

To introduce students to "The Dog of Pompeii," gather photographs, books, and pop-ups that illustrate volcanic eruptions. If possible, show students a video clip of a volcanic explosion. As a class, discuss what happens when a volcanic eruption or an earthquake occurs in a populated area.

> **TEACHER TIP**
>
> I use this activity when we read the short story "The Dog of Pompeii" by Louis Untermeyer, but it can be used with any story or novel.

OBJECTIVE: To motivate students to imagine a volcanic eruption

TIME: About 30 minutes

MATERIALS (to make one volcano)
1/2 cup flour • 1 tablespoon baking soda • 1 tablespoon vinegar • plastic bowl or a large margarine tub • red food coloring • water • paper towels

STEP-BY-STEP

1. Pour the flour into the bowl. Form the flour into the shape of a mountain.
2. Use a finger to make a depression in the top of the mountain of flour.
3. Put the baking soda inside the depression.
4. Put two drops of red food coloring on top of the baking soda.
5. Pour the vinegar over the baking soda and observe what happens.
6. Empty the plastic bowl into the trash can.
7. Clean the work area.

After students complete the experiment, ask them to do a free write. While students are writing, darken the room and show an overhead transparency of a volcanic eruption. (To create volcanic dust and ash, I sometimes clap erasers.) In the background, play a tape of a volcano exploding. Ask students to imagine that they are in Pompeii the day Mt. Vesuvius erupts. Tell them to think about and write what they would see, hear, feel, touch, and taste on the streets of Pompeii. Remind them to write about their emotions and thoughts.

After the free write, students can share their responses. Discuss students' observations and connect them to what is going to happen in the story. As they read, have them use sticky notes to mark passages that best describe the various settings.

Setting Postcards

OBJECTIVE: To respond to the author's description of setting by creating a postcard

TIME: Two 40-minute class periods, or assign as homework

MATERIALS

Postcard Rubric (page 24) • large index cards • crayons, markers, colored pencils • rulers • sample postcards

STEP-BY-STEP

1. In small groups, students take turns reading the passages they identified with sticky notes. As each student reads, the group members visualize the places described.

2. Write the directions from Postcard How-tos (right) on the board, or type the directions and distribute them. Adjust the directions to accommodate the literature your class is reading. Ask students to write a rough draft of their letters before they copy it onto the postcards. Let them peer edit their drafts. After they proofread and revise their draft, they should copy it onto the completed postcard.

3. Use the Postcard Rubric to evaluate students' work.

Postcard How-to's

Have students do the following:
ON THE LINED SIDE:

a. Using a ruler, divide the page in half.

b. In the upper right corner, create an Italian postage stamp.

c. On the right side, address the postcard to a friend or family member. Include the name, street address, city, state, and zip code.

d. Imagine that you are a tourist visiting Pompeii at the time of the story and that you are writing to a friend or relative. On the left side, describe the setting in detail. Remember to include a greeting, a closing, and a signature.

ON THE PLAIN SIDE:

e. Draw a detailed drawing of the setting. Be sure to fill in all the white space. Use crayons, markers, or colored pencils to add detail.

Dear Mom and Dad,

Hi! I'm having a great time in Pompeii! This is a busy, rich city. Yesterday we watched the chariot races. Boy! They were exciting. The chariots moved so fast they were a blur of silver and red. Following that, fireworks exploded across the sky!

Some strange, smoky smells are in the air today, and I feel a rumbling under my feet. The air is thick with dust, and Vesuvius is smoking heavily. I wonder what that red liquid is streaming down the mountainside.

Love,
Caroline

MS SALLY MILLER
691 LILAC LANE
CARLISLE, PA 17013

Setting Murals

HOW TO USE THIS ACTIVITY: You can create two murals to compare and contrast the setting of two novels, or make one mural as a panoramic view of the setting of a novel.

OBJECTIVE: To create a mural depicting the setting of a novel

TIME: Two 40-minute class periods

MATERIALS

index cards • one large sheet of white butcher paper at least 10 feet long • plastic containers half filled with water • three buckets, two empty and one filled with water (if a sink is not available in your room, pour dirty water in the empty buckets and clean brushes and containers in the water-filled bucket) • paintbrushes • tempera paint in a variety of colors • shower curtains and/or large plastic garbage bags to cover the floor • paper towels • colored markers

On the lined side of an index card, write the page number on which a student could find a description of the setting, a brief statement defining the setting, and a specific scene or object for the student to draw. Number each card on the other side.

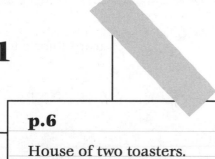

1

p.6

House of two toasters. Make an interior view of the house. You draw 2 bedrooms, each with single beds.

STEP-BY-STEP

Day 1

1. Distribute the index cards. Have students read the page describing their setting and then sketch it on scrap paper.

2. Line students up in numerical order along the butcher paper.

3. Small groups of students with related settings should plan their section of the mural and sketch it onto the butcher paper. For example, three students may be drawing Finsterwald's backyard. One student sketches the yard; another draws the house; and a third makes the "graveyard" of tennis balls, footballs, Frisbees, airplanes, and boomerangs.

4. Tell students to wear old clothes or bring a painting shirt or smock to class for tomorrow's painting activity.

Day 2

1. Before class, prepare the room for painting. Cover the floor with plastic garbage bags or newspaper. Spread the butcher paper on the floor.

2. Make six to eight painting stations along the mural. At each station, have paintbrushes, a plastic container half-filled with water, tempera paints, markers, and paper towels.

3. Have students line up in numerical order. Assign the odd numbers to go to the "ground side" of the mural and the even numbers to go to the "sky side" of the mural. While students on the "ground side" paint yesterday's sketches, students on the "sky side" paint the sky and clouds. Designate one person to paint the sun. Remind students to do the fine detail work, such as a person's face, with a marker before painting. Have students check for white space and fill it.
4. Dry and hang the mural.

VARIATION: MINI-MURALS

If you want to create small murals, divide the class into small groups. Give each group an index card with a passage describing one of the settings in the novel. Be sure each group receives a different passage. Have the group paint its mural. When the mini-murals are finished, number each one and hang them in the room. Duplicate a class set of the descriptions written on the index cards. Then have the class do a silent gallery tour of the murals in which they match the passage to the picture that represents the setting.

> **TEACHER TIP**
>
> Instead of using index cards, I type my setting passages on the computer. I print them, cut them out, and distribute them to the groups, and use the master to duplicate the class sets.

ACTIVITY 5

Life-Size Settings

HOW TO USE THIS ACTIVITY: As part of an interdisciplinary unit on oceanography, students research marine animals and study ocean life. Using the information learned in science class, students become marine animals and work in cooperative groups to write plays, puppet shows, or children's books from the animal's point of view. The purpose of these projects is to send a strong environmental message about the need to protect and preserve the ocean, the coral reef, and all of the plants and animals that inhabit it. After students complete their projects, we invite first, second, and third graders to see the student productions and presentations. To strengthen the impact of the environmental message, we create a three-dimensional setting. I've included directions for making a coral reef, but you can easily adapt this activity to create life-size settings of novels as well. For example, created the Alaskan tundra for *Julie of the Wolves* or the Canadian wilderness for *Hatchet*.

OBJECTIVE: To create a 3-D life-size setting

TIME: Preparation—Two days if you use parent volunteers

Construction—Two 40-minute class periods

Assembly—One evening with parent volunteers

MATERIALS

2' x 2' sheets of different colors of butcher paper • 3' x 3' sheets of different colors of butcher paper • 4' x 4' sheets of different colors of butcher paper • newspaper • tempera paints • lace • tissue paper • green streamers • rubber cement • sponges for sponge painting • markers • staplers • masking tape • ladders • extension cords • hot-glue guns • hot-glue sticks (last four materials are for adult use only)

STEP-BY-STEP

1. Organize a group of parent or student volunteers to precut the paper needed.
2. Demonstrate how to make 3-D plants and animals:
   a. Fold a piece of butcher paper in half.
   b. Draw the shape of the animal or plant.
   c. Cut it out, through both pieces of paper, but do not cut along the fold.
   d. Color and paint one side of the animal or plant. Add detail with markers.
   e. Stuff the plant or animal with newspaper and staple the sides together.
3. Demonstrate how to make kelp:
   a. Twist precut pieces of 4' brown butcher paper into tight vine-like structures.
   b. Make large green leaves to attach to the vines.
   c. Hot-glue the leaves to the vines.
4. Demonstrate how to make flat leaves, shells, coral, etc.:
   a. Trace one pattern.
   b. Place the pattern on top of a precut stack of butcher paper.
      Be sure the pile is not too thick to cut.
   c. Cut out six to ten objects at a time.
   d. Decorate each object separately.

TEACHER TIP

I borrow hot-glue guns from parents and staff members. Hot-glue sticks are donated from parents and local craft stores.

TEACHER TIP

Before you start this project, be sure that you can hang the butcher paper panels from the ceiling. We tuck the paper into our ceiling tiles and tape it where necessary. Practice hanging the panels to work out the glitches prior to parent volunteer night.

Measure from the ceiling to the floor of your room. Cut panels of blue and brown butcher paper to hang from the ceiling to the floor. The blue paper should be 2' longer than the brown paper. In my room, I use 6' of blue paper and 4' of brown paper. Hot glue the sheets of blue paper to the sheets of brown paper to make the 10' panels.

5. Provide books containing pictures of coral reef animals and plants so students have models for creating artwork. Divide students into groups to create the following items:
   - 3-D animals (be sure to have lots of volunteers in this group)
   - 3-D plants
   - Kelp and kelp leaves
   - Miscellaneous objects, such as shells, coral, and seaweed that are part of the background

6. When students have finished making all the materials, invite the parent volunteers to school to hot-glue all items to the large butcher-paper panels and to hang the finished panels around the room. Organize the volunteers into the following groups:
   a. Panel planners—decorate one panel at a time with sea creatures, plants, etc.
   b. Gluers—glue the objects on the panels into place.
   c. Sponge painters—add bubbles and color to the ocean and objects.
   d. Hangers—hang the finished panels (practice with a plain panel first to avoid tearing).
   e. Tapers—use masking tape to tape the backs of the panels together; tape seaweed streamers to the bottom of the panels.
   f. Cleanup crew—help clean up and set up the room.

7. When the coral reef is complete, ask students to bring beach towels to class. Use the environment for creative writing activities and for the presentations to the elementary students.

TECHNOLOGY CONNECTION

Compare and contrast the setting in a story or a novel to the "real" place. Have students research a specific location on the Internet. Encourage them to contact the bureau of tourism in the area to send pamphlets, brochures, and other information. If possible, have students e-mail a class in the area to get firsthand information about life in the region.

Setting Pop-up Directions

GROUP MEMBERS' NAMES   DATE_____

_____, _____,

_____, _____

GROUP ROLES

1. *Geographer/Gopher*   Locate the setting of the novel in the atlas or on a map. Get all of the materials the group needs to construct the pop-up page. Return all the materials at the end of the period.

2. *Locator #1/Taskmaster* Find one passage in the novel that describes the setting of the novel. Write it on your index card. Keep the group focused and on task.

3. *Locator #2/ Checker*   Find a second passage in the novel that describes the setting. Write it on an index card. Read the directions below to your group. Check off each item as it is completed.

4. *Locator #3/ Encourager* Find a third passage that describes your setting. Write it on an index card. Give your group positive feedback.

ALL GROUP MEMBERS   Each person in the group must contribute one item to the pop-up page.

DIRECTIONS FOR MAKING THE POP-UP PAGE

___ **1.** Number yourselves from 1 to 4.

___ **2.** Assign the group roles listed above.

___ **3.** The Geographer/Gopher shares the geographic setting in the atlas or on the map.

___ **4.** Each Locator writes a setting passage on an index card and reads it aloud to the group. Before writing the passage check with other Locators to be sure everyone has a different passage. Group members visualize or picture the setting as it is described.

___ **5.** Discuss what you want to include on your pop-up page.

___ **6.** Draw a sketch of your design.

___ **7.** Get the materials you need to construct the pop-up.

___ **8.** To make the pop-up, follow the directions below:

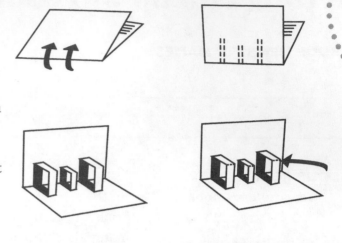

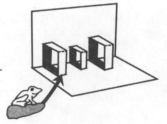

a. Fold the oak tag in half. Make a smooth, even crease.

b. Use a ruler to draw the tabs on which you will glue each object that "pops up." The tabs should be at least 1" long but no longer than 1 1/2". The tabs should be between 1/2" and 1" wide.

c. If you want to use a different color paper for the background, glue that paper onto the oak tag *before* you cut the tabs.

d. Cut the tabs on the vertical lines only.

e. Open the folded paper. Pull the tabs inside and crease the fold to make the background stand up.

f. Add details to the background, foreground, and middle ground. Make pop-up pieces that portray your setting. Glue the pop-up pieces onto the page.

___ **9.** Each person in the group must produce at least one item for the pop-up page.

___ **10.** In addition to the pop-up display, make sure your group has three index cards with passages that describe the setting. Include a fourth index card that has your group members' names, the date, and the section on it. This is a graded project.

Setting Pop-Up Rubric

GROUP MEMBERS' NAMES   **DATE**_____

_____, _____,

_____, _____

Before you give the rubric to the teacher, score the project as a group. Circle the appropriate number for each criterion and then record your score where it says *Group Score*.

1 The index cards contain three quotations from the story that clearly describe an important setting.

4   The three quotations clearly describe the major setting in the story.

3   The three quotations relate to the setting but miss one important point.

2   Quotations somewhat relate to the setting but are not key passages, or one quotation is missing.

1   Quotations do not relate to the novel's major setting, or two quotations are missing.

Group Score: _____   Teacher's Score: _____

2 The pop-up effectively represents the setting described on the index card and in the story.

4   The pop-up definitely represents the setting described in the quotations.

3   The pop-up includes most of the information contained in the quotations.

2   The pop-up includes some of the information contained in the quotations.

1   The pop-up does not resemble the story's setting.

Group Score: _____   Teacher's Score: _____

3 The description of setting includes both time and place.

4   The time and place are clearly identified.

3   Time and place are identified but could be more specific.

2   Only time or place is identified.

1   Neither time nor place is identified.

Group Score: _____   Teacher's Score: _____

4 **The pop-up is effectively planned, creative, and colorful.**

    4   The pop-up is effectively planned, and is creative and colorful.

    3   The pop-up is organized and is somewhat creative and colorful.

    2   The pop-up needs more organization, creativity, and color.

    1   The pop-up looks as if it were thrown together at the last minute.

Group Score: _____   Teacher's Score: _____

5 **Each group member contributed one or more items to the pop-up.**

    4   Each group member contributed.

    3   Most group members contributed.

    2   A few group members contributed.

    1   One group member did most of the work.

Group Score: _____   Teacher's Score: _____

Total Points Possible: 20   **Total Points Earned:** _____

Setting Cinquain and Watercolor Rubric

Rating Scale	4	3	2	1	NR
	excellent	good	fair	needs improvement	not ready

Circle the appropriate rating level for each of the criteria listed below. Total all of the points to determine the score.

Criteria	Rating Scale
1. Uses correct cinquain form.	4 3 2 1 NR
2. Cinquain contains vivid verbs and powerful adjectives.	4 3 2 1 NR
3. Poem accurately describes setting.	4 3 2 1 NR
4. Words are spelled correctly.	4 3 2 1 NR
5. Watercolor accurately represents the setting described in the story.	4 3 2 1 NR
6. Painting includes background, foreground, and middle ground.	4 3 2 1 NR
7. Watercolor effectively uses wash techniques demonstrated in class.	4 3 2 1 NR
8. Painting uses at least one of the following techniques to add detail:	4 3 2 1 NR

- colored pencils
- pastel
- dry brush
- outlining

9. The painting is properly framed.	4 3 2 1 NR
10. All work is neat.	4 3 2 1 NR
11. The final product demonstrates time and effort were put into the project.	4 3 2 1 NR

Total Points Possible: 44   **Total Points Earned: _____**

Students receiving an NR must resubmit their product after improving it.

Postcard Rubric

NAME _____ **DATE** _____ **SECTION** _____

Circle the appropriate rating level for each criteria listed below. Total the points to determine the score.

Criteria	Outstanding	Good	Acceptable
Colorful illustration that accurately shows the story's setting.	4	3	2
All parts are correctly placed.	4	3	2
All parts use correct form.	4	3	2
The message describes the setting.	4	3	2
Correct capitalization.	4	3	2
Correct punctuation.	4	3	2
Neat, readable writing.	4	3	2
Accurate spelling.	4	3	2
Complete sentences.	4	3	2

Total Points Possible: 36   **Total Points Earned:** _____

Postcard could be mailed: **Yes**   **No**

(If the answer is yes, you will receive 2 bonus points toward your grade.)

❑ The check mark in this box means that your postcard is not ready to be graded. Improve its quality and then give it to your teacher. If you are not sure how to improve your postcard, talk to your teacher.

Student Comments

The best part of my postcard is

_____

_____

I need to improve

_____

_____

By making this postcard I learned

_____

_____

CHAPTER 2

Character

The Purpose of the Character Activities

Reader response theory suggests that for readers to comprehend and interpret text, they need to make personal connections to the story and share these responses with other readers (Beers and Samuels 1998). To connect with the characters in a novel, readers need to be aware of associations, feelings, and attitudes they have toward the characters (Beers and Samuels 1998). One way to help students actively engage with the characters is to use a reader response journal that encourages students to carefully observe them.

Ask students to set aside five or more pages in their reader response journals to use as a character log. Tell them to fold each page in half and draw a line down the middle. Title the left-hand side of each page "What the Text Says." Have students jot down what the main character says, does, thinks, and feels. In addition, tell students to describe what other characters say about the protagonist and how they interact with him or her. Title the right-hand side of each page "My Response to the Character." On this side of the log, students write their personal reactions and feelings toward the character. They also record ways they resemble or differ from the protagonist.

Later, students can share their reactions to the characters in literature discussion groups. To demonstrate what they have learned, have students engage in hands-on activities designed to help them further analyze the characters.

WHAT THE TEXT SAYS	MY RESPONSE TO THE CHARACTER
"'Angel face,' the other boys called [Rudi]. Or rather had called him, until they learned that his fists, though small, were useful. Most of the men of Kurtal had black hair. Rudi had blond. Most of them had dark eyes. Rudi's were light …"	Like Rudi, I am different from most kids. They tease me because I am tall and have big feet. Unlike Rudi, I am not very coordinated. I too stand up for myself, but I don't use my fists. I carry myself with respect. When someone bullies me, I ignore him. If I were to meet Rudi Matt, I think we could be friends.

An Introduction to Characterization

Introduce characterization by writing the name of a character students know, such as Cinderella, on the chalkboard. Then ask students to give as much information as they can to help a stranger become acquainted with her. List students' responses and explain that they reveal how an author creates a character. After providing time for students to study the board, have them write down several methods they think an author uses to develop a character.

First, have partners share their written responses, then discuss characterization as a class. Lead students to see that an author creates a character by portraying what the character looks like, says, does, thinks, and feels. In addition, how the character interacts with others and what others say about him or her also provide important information.

Next, write the name of a character from your current story or novel on the board. Students should use their novels to find examples of the character's words, actions, thoughts, and feelings that reveal information about his or her personality. In small groups, have students share the passages and analyze what they say about the character.

ACTIVITY I

Life-Size Characters

HOW TO USE THIS ACTIVITY:
Because the final product is life-size, create the characters in cooperative groups. Since the project involves an in-depth look at a character, use it with novels instead of short stories. If the whole class is reading the same novel, assign different characters to different groups, or allow each group to choose one of the characters. If reading different novels, ask groups to use the protagonist as their character.

OBJECTIVES: To create a visual representation of a character; to analyze a character

TIME: Three to four 40-minute class periods

MATERIALS

large sheets of butcher paper 5' or 6' long • construction paper • markers and crayons • rulers • scissors • glue sticks • Life-Size Character Analysis and Life-Size Character Rubric reproducibles (pages 34–36)

STEP-BY-STEP

1. Assign or have groups choose a character from the novel they are reading.
2. Number group members 1 to 4 and tell them to assume the following group roles:

   1. ***Character's Voice:*** Look for examples of the character's speech that reveal important information about him or her. Record at least two direct quotes. Beneath each quote, record what you think the character's words say about him or her.

   2. ***Character's Deeds:*** Search for passages that show something the character does. Write at least two examples of the character's actions. Use direct quotes, or state what the character does in your own words. Beneath each statement, record what you think the character's actions reveal about him or her.

   3. ***Character's Looks:*** Find passages that describe the character's appearance. If you cannot find a direct quote, write what you think the character looks like and why you picture the character this way. Include information about the character's hair color, eye color, age, height, and distinguishing features. Draw a sketch of the character.

   4. ***Character's Thoughts and Feelings:*** Find descriptions of the character's thoughts and feelings. Record at least two passages that show what's inside the character's mind and heart. Beneath each quote, record what you learn about the character by examining his or her thoughts or feelings.

3. Distribute copies of the Life-Size Character Analysis reproducible and ask each student to complete the section that corresponds to his or her group role. If one group member finishes before another, he or she can assist other group members.
4. Tell group members to make suggestions for improvement and peer edit each other's work.
5. As a group, students discuss similarities and differences between themselves and the character. Then one group member completes "The Character and Me" section of the reproducible on page 34.
6. Next, a volunteer lies down in the middle of the butcher paper to be traced. After the tracing is completed, group members outline the shape in black marker and erase any pencil marks.
7. Working cooperatively, students add clothes and facial features to the "body" to portray the character studied. They may work from the sketch drawn by the "Character's Looks" group member.
8. Students cut the shapes from Life-Size Character Analysis reproducible and glue them onto the butcher paper. Students glue "The Character and Me" to the bottom of the butcher paper.
9. Each group introduces its life-size character to the class. The class then compares and contrasts the various characters.
10. Use the Life-Size Character Rubric (pages 35–36) to evaluate students' work.

Character Suitcase

HOW TO USE THIS ACTIVITY: This activity is quite versatile. It can be used with short or long works of literature, and it can be an individual or a group activity. Use it to assess a student's knowledge of a character.

OBJECTIVE: To interpret a character by packing a suitcase with tangible and intangible items the character might take on a trip

TIME: Two or three 40-minute class periods, or assign as homework

MATERIALS

small cardboard boxes to use for suitcases • construction paper • markers, crayons, colored pencils • glue sticks • scissors • fabric scraps • stickers • computer art

STEP-BY-STEP

1. Explain that students will make and pack a suitcase that one of the characters in a story or novel will take on a trip. They need to include the following items (objects may be handmade, computer art, stickers, or small objects):

   a. A luggage tag that has the character's name, address, and destination written on it.

   b. Memorabilia to decorate the outside of the suitcase, such as bumper stickers or mementos from previous trips.

   > **TEACHER TIP**
   >
   > Two weeks before beginning the project, ask students to collect small boxes that resemble a suitcase or carry-on luggage. If students have extra boxes, put these in the classroom donation bin. (I use the copy paper boxes from the office.) Students who do not have a box can make their suitcase from construction paper.

   c. Ten items that the character would pack. These items may be both tangible and intangible. For example, Brian Robeson, the main character in *Hatchet*, packs a hatchet (tangible) and courage (intangible) because he needs both to survive.

   d. A brief explanation stating why the character chose to pack each item. It should be written from the character's point of view. The example on the following page may be used as a model for students.

Brian Robeson's Suitcase

Given the last experience I had when visiting my dad in the Canadian wilderness I know what to pack for this trip. Last summer the pilot of the Cessna 406 had a fatal heart attack, and the plane crashed, stranding me in the middle of the wilderness. I vowed to get my pilot's license, which I now have.

I'm packing my hatchet because it was my lifeline last summer. For luck, I'm taking a twenty-dollar bill just in case I need it for tinder. I'm also bringing a compass to help me find my way home, a sleeping bag to stay warm, and a tent to provide shelter. Since water is essential, I'll carry a canteen, for I might not find a lake this time. If I run into another porcupine, a first aid kit will make it easier to disinfect and bandage the wounds.

To remind me not to lose hope, I'll light a candle every night. When I lost hope last summer, I became so depressed I almost died. I'll also pack the medal for bravery my hometown gave me upon my return; courage is definitely needed in the wilderness.
To keep me from feeling lonely and isolated, I'll bring along a picture of my best friend, Terry. Now I'm ready to go. I hope this trip to Dad's is uneventful, but just in case, I'm prepared.

2. In small groups, have students share their suitcases. If students are reading different books or novels, form jigsaw groups so students can teach each other about different characters.

Paper-Chain Characters

HOW TO USE THIS ACTIVITY:

Paper-Chain Characters help a student analyze a character in a story and also serve to compare and contrast the character with themselves.

This activity works best if completed individually. Students may make paper chains of the protagonist of the stories or novels you are studying.

OBJECTIVE: To create a paper chain that analyzes a character and makes a personal connection between the reader and the character

TIME: Two 40-minute class periods, or assign as homework

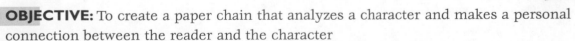

MATERIALS

18" x 12" white construction paper • colored construction paper • rulers • scissor • markers, crayons, colored pencils • glue sticks

STEP-BY-STEP

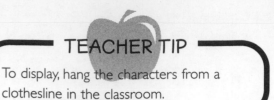
1. Tell students to hold the white construction paper horizontally. Have them draw four vertical lines approximately 3 9/16" apart.

2. Show students how to fold the paper accordion-style along the lines.

3. Have students draw the shape of the character on the folded paper. They should make sure that the feet and hands touch the folds.

4. Next ask them to cut out the areas between the arms, legs, and head. Make sure students do not cut the folds around the hands and feet.

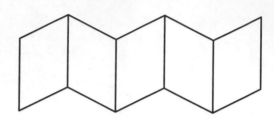

5. Finally, unfold the paper. They should have five characters in the paper chain.

6. On the front of the first paper character, ask students to draw details to portray the character based on his or her description in the story. On the back of the first paper character, they draw a picture of themselves. They may want to add construction paper details. (Do not use dark markers, or the colors will bleed through.)

7. On the front of the second paper character, students write the character's favorite saying or one of his or her important quotes. On the back, they write their own favorite saying or a quote that they especially enjoy.

8. On the front of the third paper character, students write what the character does or how he or she acts. On the back, they write what they like to do.

9. On the front of the fourth paper character, write what someone in the novel says about the character. On the back of the fourth paper character, write what their friends would say about them.

10. On the front of the fifth paper character, students write the character's likes and dislikes. On the back, they write their own likes and dislikes.

11. Students can add color and design to the paper chain.

12. Encourage students to share the paper chain with a partner.

Caricatures

HOW TO USE THIS ACTIVITY:

Use caricatures to introduce exaggeration as an element of such legends as Paul Bunyan or Maniac Magee. For homework, have students look through old magazines and newspapers to find examples of political caricatures. Share and display these pictures in class.

"They say Maniac Magee was born in a dump. They say his stomach was a cereal box and his heart a sofa spring."

Next, have students investigate the legend's text to find descriptions of exaggeration. Specifically, have them search for larger-than-life portraits of the characters, such as "They say Maniac Magee was born in a dump. They say his stomach was a cereal box and his heart a sofa spring." To facilitate the process of finding the quotations, list the characters' names on the board and cite pages to which the students can refer. Have students use sticky notes to mark passages that are examples of exaggeration.

In small groups, ask students to share their findings. As they listen to the descriptions, students visualize the characters and then share their mental pictures with the group.

OBJECTIVES: To use the author's verbal exaggeration to visualize the character in the story and to draw a caricature based on this written description

TIME: Two 40-minute class periods, or assign as homework

MATERIALS

cartooning books • illustrated tall tale books • white construction paper • crayons, markers, colored pencils • sticky notes

STEP-BY-STEP

1. Have students locate the exaggerated description of the character.
2. Have them use the cartooning books and the examples of caricatures to help decide what features they will exaggerate.
3. Tell them to sketch the caricature on scrap paper.
4. Then ask students to draw and color the final copy on white construction paper.
5. Beneath the picture, they should write the quote from the story that inspired the caricature.

> ### TEACHER TIP
>
> I use this activity with *Maniac Magee*. As an anticipatory set, I read Steven Kellogg's retelling of *Paul Bunyan*, and the class discusses the effect of exaggeration in this tale.

Collaborative Character Map

HOW TO USE THIS ACTIVITY: Ask groups of students to create a character map for the protagonist of the novel. After the project is completed, have each group share its map. Then use a matrix to compare and contrast the main characters. This activity can also be used as an individual project that is completed as a homework or in-class assignment.

OBJECTIVES: To analyze the main character of a story or novel by constructing a character map; to use a matrix to compare and contrast various characters

TIME: Two to three 40-minute class periods

MATERIALS

12" x 18" white construction paper • markers, crayons, colored pencils • scissors • glue sticks • dictionaries, thesauruses • Collaborative Character Map Directions, Collaborative Character Map Drafting Sheet, Character Matrix, and Comparing and Contrasting Characters reproducibles (pages 37–40) • overhead transparency of the Character Matrix (page 39)

STEP-BY-STEP

1. Number group members 1 to 4 and tell them to assume the following group roles:
   1. *Encourager:* Compliment the group and encourage everyone to work together to complete the job.
   2. *Sheriff:* Get the materials for the group; keep everyone on task.
   3. *Reader/Checker:* Read the instructions to the group and check off each item as it is completed.
   4. *Recorder:* On the back of the map, write down two ways the main character changes.
2. Distribute one copy of the Collaborative Character Map Directions and Collaborative Character Map Drafting Sheet to each group.
3. Tell students that they are going to work in groups to discuss the character traits of the protagonist and to complete the draft of the character map. Each person in the group is responsible for creating one section of the map. On the "spokes" of each branch, students write vivid, precise nouns or adjectives that describe the protagonist's major character traits. Emphasize the importance of selecting the best words to describe the heart of the protagonist's personality. Point out that students should not use dull words, such as *good* or *nice*, and suggest using a thesaurus as a reference tool. Explain that in the boxes attached to the spokes students are to write evidence to support their choice of adjectives.

Evidence consists of:

- What the character says—a quotation

- What the character does—a description of the character's important actions

- What other characters say about him or her—a quotation

- How the character interacts with others—a description or a quotation

Explain that in the center of the character map, students need to put symbols that represent the main character. For example, to show the pain Karana, from *Island of the Blue Dolphins*, experiences when her tribe leaves and wild dogs kill her brother Ramo, students might place a broken heart, a tombstone, and a ship in the center of the map. Ask students to discuss possible symbols for their characters in their groups.

4. Once the groups have discussed the words, evidence, and symbols they will use to describe the protagonist, ask them to complete a draft using the other reproducible. Remind them to use a dictionary to check the spelling.

5. After students complete the draft, have them discuss how the protagonist changed during the story. Ask the Recorder to write two major changes on the back of the draft.

6. Review the students' drafts and provide feedback. When the drafts have been approved, the group completes the final copy.

7. When presenting the character maps to the class, each group member individually shares his or her section.

8. After all of the groups have shared the character maps, use the overhead transparency of the Character Matrix to complete it as a class. Distribute individual copies of the matrix to students so they can record the data. Use the following procedures:
   a. List the main characters in the left-hand column under "Character."
   b. List character traits or qualities of one character across the top of the grid.
   c. Fill in the grid, using plus (+) when a character exhibits the trait and minus (–) when the character does not exhibit the trait.

9. When the grid is complete, ask students to individually complete the Comparing and Contrasting Characters reproducible.

Life-Size Character Analysis

NAME _____ **DATE** _____ **SECTION** _____

CHARACTER'S NAME _____

Character's Voice

What the character says:

_____

_____

_____

Character's Voice

What the words show:

_____

_____

_____

_____

Character's Deeds

What the character does:

_____

_____

_____

_____

Character's Deeds

What the actions show:

_____

_____

_____

_____

Character's Thoughts and Feelings

What the character thinks and feels:

_____

_____

_____

Character's Thoughts and Feelings

What the thoughts and feelings show:

_____

_____

_____

_____

Character's Looks

Hair color: _____ Eye color: _____

Age: _____ Height: _____

Distinguishing features: _____

_____

The Character and Me

Similarities: _____

_____

Differences: _____

_____

Life-Size Character Rubric

Circle the appropriate number for each criterion listed below. Add all the numbers to determine the score.

1 The character looks the way the book describes him or her; the details are factually accurate.

    4   The character looks exactly the way the novel describes him or her.

    3   The character resembles the novel's description.

    2   The character somewhat resembles the description in the novel.

    1   The character does not resemble the description in the novel.

2 The character's words convey his or her thoughts, beliefs, personality, and/or attitude.

    4   Quotations provide deep insight into the character.

    3   Quotations illustrate important character traits.

    2   Quotations provide minor insights into the character.

    1   Quotations provide little insight into the character.

3 The interpretations of the character's words demonstrate an understanding of his or her traits.

    4   Interpretations show a clear, accurate understanding of the character.

    3   Interpretations show a solid understanding of the character.

    2   Interpretations show some understanding of the character.

    1   Interpretations show little understanding of the character.

4 The character's behavior is clearly demonstrated in the actions selected.

    4   Actions definitely reveal character's personality, attitude, and/or beliefs.

    3   Actions reveal character's personality, attitude, and/or beliefs.

    2   Actions somewhat reveal character's personality, attitude, and/or beliefs.

    1   Actions do not reveal character's personality, attitude, and/or beliefs.

5 The interpretations of the character's actions demonstrate an understanding of the character's traits.

    4   Interpretations show a clear, accurate understanding of the character.

    3   Interpretations show a solid understanding of the character.

    2   Interpretations show some understanding of the character.

    1   Interpretations show little understanding of the character.

6 Passages selected to reveal the character's thoughts and feelings reveal important aspects of his or her inner self.

4 Passages provide a bird's-eye view of the character's inner self.

3 Passages provide insight into the character's inner self.

2 Passages show some insight into the character's inner self.

1 Passages show little insight into the character's inner self.

7 Interpretations of text related to the character's thoughts and feelings demonstrate an understanding of the character's mind and heart.

4 Interpretations show a clear, accurate understanding of the character's mind and heart.

3 Interpretations show a solid understanding of the character's mind and heart.

2 Interpretations show some understanding of the character's mind and heart.

1 Interpretations show little understanding of the character's mind and heart.

8 Comparisons of self to character are clear, show strong personal connections, and reveal insight into the character.

4 Clear, strong, insightful comparisons.

3 Clear, insightful comparisons.

2 Comparisons are moderately insightful and somewhat clear.

1 Unclear comparisons that have little insight.

9 The quotations, passages, and interpretations clearly show the heart of the character's personality.

4 The character's personality is clearly and effectively portrayed.

3 The character's personality is well defined.

2 The character's personality is somewhat clear.

1 The character's personality is not clearly or effectively presented.

10 The project is organized and neat, and provides a clear portrait of the novel's character.

4 Very neat, organized, and definitely helps the reader understand the character.

3 Neat, organized, and helps the reader know the character better.

2 Fairly neat, somewhat organized, and presents a fuzzy picture of the character.

1 Messy, disorganized, and presents an unclear picture of the character.

Grading Scale: 40–37 = A   36–35 = B   34–31 = C   30–28 = D
Below 28 = Not ready yet. Resubmit

Total Points: _____   **Final Grade:** _____

Collaborative Character Map Directions

NAME _____ **DATE** _____ **SECTION** _____

___ 1. Assign the following group roles:

   1. Encourager: Encourage everyone to work together to complete the job.

   2. Sheriff: Get the materials and keep the group on task.

   3. Reader/Checker: Read the directions aloud and check off each item as it is completed.

   4. Recorder: On the back of the map, write two ways the main character changes.

___ 2. The Encourager writes the name of the character in the center of the Collaborative Character Map Drafting Sheet.

___ 3. Discuss your character's traits or qualities. Choose the best words to describe your character. Use vivid language that describes the heart of your character's personality. Avoid dull, boring, lifeless words like *good* or *nice.*

___ 4. Fill in character's traits or qualities on the map. Spell correctly. Points will be deducted for misspelled words.

___ 5. Discuss the evidence that proves the traits or qualities you wrote down. For evidence, use:

   What the character says—a quotation

   What the character does—a description of the character's important actions

   What other characters say about him or her—a quotation

   How the character interacts with others—a description or a quotation

___ 6. Fill in the evidence on the map.

___ 7. Discuss how the character changes in the story. On the back of the map, the Recorder writes the changes your group thinks are important.

___ 8. Decide on a central symbol that represents your character.

___ 9. Have the Encourager bring the draft to the teacher for editing.

___ 10. The Sheriff collects supplies, and each group member makes and illustrates one branch of the map.

___ 11. Group presentation. Each group member shares his or her branch with the class. One member explains the significance of the central symbol. The Recorder states how the character changed.

Collaborative Character Map Drafting Sheet

GROUP MEMBERS' NAMES

DATE _____

_____, _____,

_____, _____,

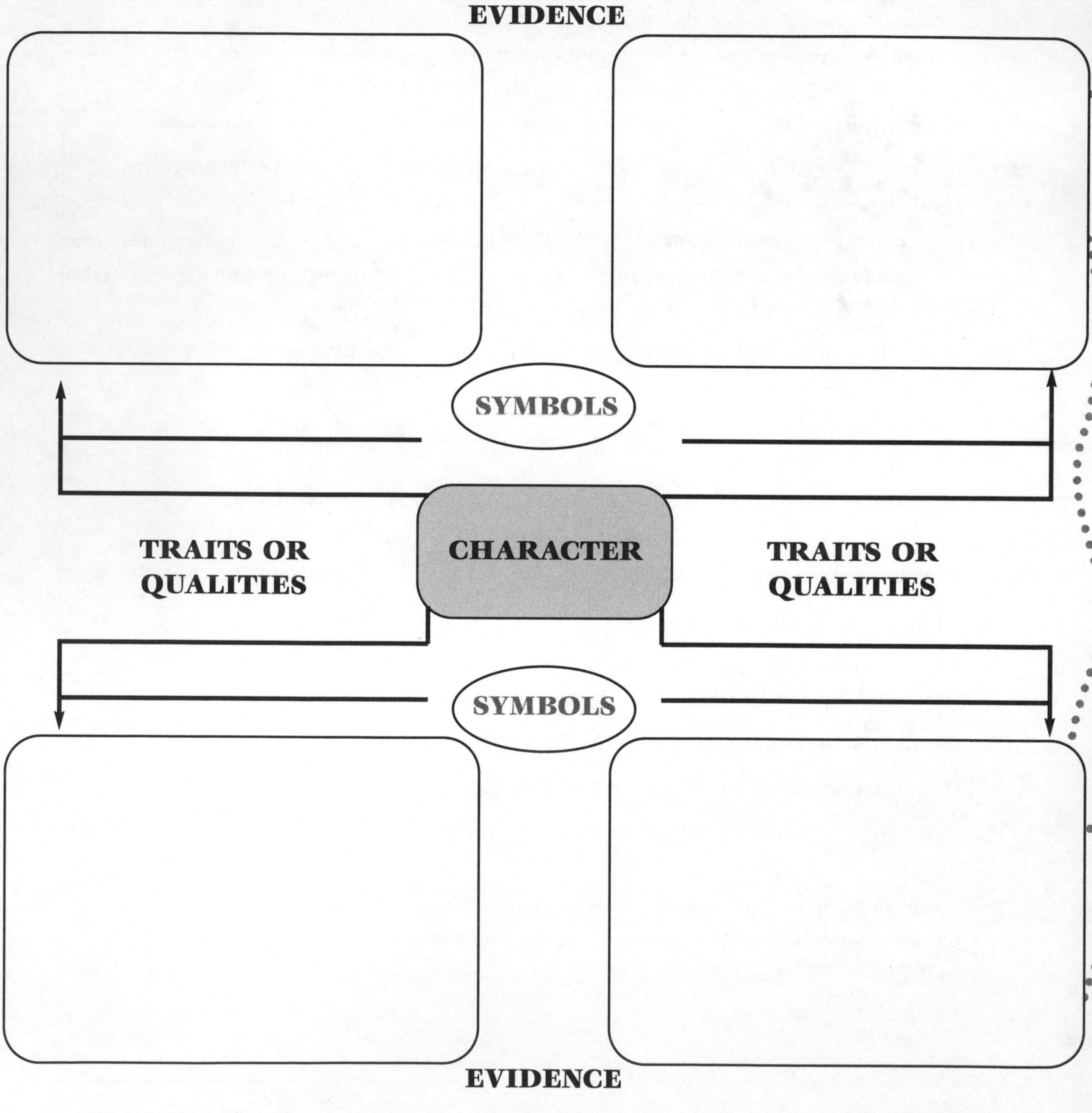

EVIDENCE

SYMBOLS

TRAITS OR QUALITIES   CHARACTER   **TRAITS OR QUALITIES**

SYMBOLS

EVIDENCE

Character Matrix

NAME _____ DATE _____ SECTION _____

Character	Traits		

Comparing and Contrasting Characters

NAME _____ **DATE** _____ **SECTION** _____

1. According to the matrix, what character traits do all of the protagonists have in common?

_____

_____

_____

2. Why do you think the main characters share common character traits?

_____

_____

_____

3. Which two characters are the most different?

_____

_____

_____

4. Why do you think these characters are so different from one another?

_____

_____

_____

5. What character traits do you and the main character of your novel share? How do you differ from one another?

_____

_____

_____

CHAPTER 3

Plot

The Purpose of the Plot Activities

Before students can interpret and critically respond to text, they must have a basic understanding of the story. Story maps and plot diagrams help students focus on essential information and recall the important events in the story (PDE 1998). Having students design and actively participate in creating story maps assists them in developing knowledge of text structure (Moore et al. 1989). Furthermore, "instruction that focuses on text structure will improve comprehension" (Beers and Samuels 1998). Story maps and plot diagrams also help students retell the story, which strengthens comprehension (Moore et al. 1989). Story maps and plot diagrams may be used to teach summarizing and to enhance students' knowledge of the art of composing a good story (Moore et al. 1989).

An Introduction to Plot

To introduce students to the concept of plot, draw a plot diagram on the board: Ask students if they are familiar with a plot diagram. Ask how this diagram might relate to the plot of a story. When students respond, "The story has a beginning, middle, and an end," say, "Yes, but what starts the story? What gets the action rolling?"

Ask a student to role-play a conflict with you. Explain that a child has received an F on his or her report card. You play the part of the parent and the student plays the part of the failing child. Get into a full-blown shouting match, and then freeze. Through questioning, lead students to discover that a story needs an initiating conflict (a problem that starts the action in the story), rising action, a climax, falling action, and a resolution.

The term *initiating conflict* is difficult for some students. Explain that it means "starting problem." Also point out that the word *solution* is contained within *resolution*. Students then make the connection that the resolution is the solution to the story problem. Remind students that stories do not always have a positive resolution and that some stories never resolve the problem.

To reinforce plot structure terminology, use the bodily-kinesthetic intelligence. When you say *plot*, have students respond with the following phrases and gestures described in the box at the right. Repeat the phrases and gestures several times until students can do them independently.

TEACHER TIP

Phrase	Gesture
plot	squat on the floor with hands folded together and pointed upward
rising action	slowly rise to a standing position; hands remain folded and pointed upward
climax	stand on tiptoes and point folded hands skyward
falling action	lean body and folded hands to the right
resolution	lean as far right as possible; touch the floor with folded hands

As students read a short story, have them identify the five parts of the plot. List the steps on a plot diagram (Initiating Conflict, Rising Action, Climax, Falling Action, Resolution) on the board or an overhead transparency. Through questioning and discussion, complete the plot diagram together. After reading a second short story, have students work in small groups to complete a plot diagram. After students read a third story, ask them to independently complete the diagram. Thus they move through the continuum of direct instruction, guided practice, and independent practice. After students have a basic understanding of plot structure, engage in hands-on activities.

ACTIVITY 1

Building Block Plot Lines

HOW TO USE THIS ACTIVITY: Because the "brain understands best when facts and skills are embedded in spatial memory" (Caine and Caine 1990), creating activities that involve building or constructing is paramount.

Have students use building materials, such as Legos, Tinkertoys, or Lincoln Logs, to create plot lines. This activity works well with *Breaker's Bridge* by Laurence Yep, but you can adapt it to other novels. Instead of building a bridge, ask students to build an object that serves as an important symbol in the novel. After they analyze the plot of the novel, they use the symbol to represent the plot line. You may also want to have students use the building materials to construct the traditional mountain-like model of the plot diagram.

OBJECTIVES: To analyze the plot of *Breaker's Bridge*; to construct Breaker's bridge and use it to represent the different elements of plot; to visualize the major symbol in the story and vicariously experience the protagonist's difficulty building the bridge

TIME: Two 40-minute class periods; assign the reading for homework

MATERIALS

sticky notes • white copy paper for sketching the bridge • white, blue, pink, yellow, and green index cards • transparent tape • building material (such as blocks or Legos) • Plot Diagram Questions for *Breaker's Bridge* and *Breaker's Bridge* Plot Activity Instruction Sheet reproducibles (pages 51 and 52)

STEP-BY-STEP

1. Draw a plot diagram on the board. Review the five parts of plot with students.
2. To set the purpose for reading and for the lesson, tell students that they are reading to identify and understand the plot of the story. Explain to students that setting is also important to this story and influences the plot. As they read, ask them to use sticky notes to mark the passages that describe the setting of the story.
3. Number group members 1 to 4 and tell them to assume the following group roles:
   1. Initiating Conflict
   2. Rising Action
   3. Climax and Resolution
   4. Falling Action

Distribute the Plot Diagram Questions (page 51). Each group member is responsible for answering the questions that correspond to his or her group role.

4. Have individual students sketch the bridge based on its description in the story.

5. Distribute *Breaker's Bridge* Plot Activity Instruction Sheet (page 52). Let group members share their responses to the questions and together check the answers for accuracy and thoroughness. By the end of the discussion, students will have summarized the story.

6. Then have students share the setting passages they marked with sticky notes. Tell students that as they listen to the passages being read, they should form a mental picture of the place being described. Have students share their sketches of the bridge and discuss which one they think is most authentic.

STEP-BY-STEP DIRECTIONS FOR THE BRIDGE-BUILDING ACTIVITY

1. Assign the group roles listed below and explain that the goal for this activity is to construct Breaker's bridge and to use the bridge to represent the different elements of plot.

    1. *Gopher:* Retrieve and return the materials.
    2. *Encourager:* Compliment the group and encourage everyone to work together to get the job done.
    3. *Reporter:* Describe the bridge and share one part of the plot with the class.
    4. *Taskmaster:* Keep the group on task and read the group instruction sheet, checking off each item as it is completed.

2. Tell students to write the events of the plot on the appropriate index card(s):
    - Initiating Conflict—white index card
    - Rising Action—pink
    - Climax—blue
    - Falling Action—green
    - Resolution—yellow

3. Explain that students are to use the sketches, information from the setting passages in the story, and the building materials to build Breaker's bridge.

4. After students construct the bridge, tell them to tape the index cards to the bridge so that the bridge represents the plot line of the story.

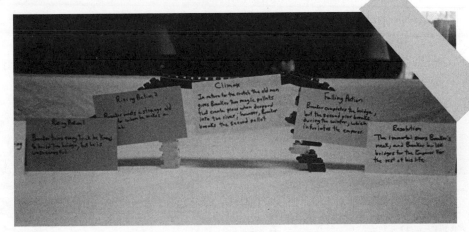

5. Have the Reporter from each group describe the group's bridge, explain how it resembles Breaker's, and state one part of the plot. Check for agreement and understanding by a show of hands from other group members each time a Reporter presents his or her information.

6. Allow groups to tour the room to see the various bridges. The class should then discuss which bridge they believe is most authentic and why.

7. Ask students to write what the bridge comes to symbolize or represent in the story. They must support their statements with evidence from the text. Share and discuss the responses.

Plot Mini-Books, Cartoons, Graphic Organizers

HOW TO USE THIS ACTIVITY:

Many students have difficulty sequencing events and separating the main events in the story from extraneous details. Consequently, they need lots of guided practice before they can independently analyze the plot of a story.

After students read *Dragon, Dragon* by John Gardner, distribute copies of the Plot Diagram. (page 53) In cooperative groups, using the round-table method, students take turns discussing the main events in the story.

As each person contributes his or her event, the group evaluates the response. When the group reaches a consensus, each member writes the event in the appropriate section of the plot diagram. To stimulate thinking during the discussion, write the following questions on the board:

- What is the initiating conflict?
- What happens as a result of this conflict?
- What is the climax or turning point of the story?
- How is the story problem solved?

Next, students choose one of three plot projects to complete independently. They may create a plot cartoon, graphic organizer, or a mini-book. Although the basic requirements are the same for these projects, they relate to different learning styles. The cartoon addresses the spatial intelligence; the graphic organizer considers the logical-mathematical intelligence, and the mini-book appeals to the linguistic intelligence. Before students begin the projects, model examples of all three and set high standards for the quality of work. These activities may be used with any short story or novel.

OBJECTIVES: To identify accurately the five parts of the plot; to identify and sequence the main events in the story

TIME: Assign as homework; give students three or more nights to complete the project

MATERIALS

ruler • white copy paper • 8" x 12" white construction paper • 11" x 17" drawing paper • scissors • thin, fine blue or black pen *or* very sharp pencil • colored pencils, markers, or crayons • literature books • Plot Diagram reproducible (page 53)

TEACHER TIP

I allow the students to use the computer and clip art to complete the project.

MINI-BOOK STEP-BY-STEP

1. Encourage students to make a rough draft of the mini-book before doing their final work. Each of the following items must be included in the mini-book:

   a. A colorfully illustrated cover that includes the title of the story and the author's name

   b. The initiating conflict

   c. Events in the rising action

   d. The climax

   e. Events in the falling action

   f. The resolution

   g. Colorful illustrations that relate to the text on each page

   h. Student's name and date

2. Have students fold the construction paper as shown in the illustration.

3. With the fold at the top, they fold the paper in half horizontally, like the pages of a book.

4. Then they fold the paper in half horizontally again, like the pages of a book.

5. Tell students to open the booklet up so that four long boxes face them.

6. Then they cut a thin line directly on the fold between the middle two boxes.

7. Have students stand the paper up and make a sharp crease on both of the center fold lines.

8. Then students place the thumb and fingers of each hand on the ends of the booklet. Push the ends of the paper together until they touch.

9. They firmly crease the spine of the booklet (the exterior center fold) to form the mini-book.

10. Finally, tell them to trim any uneven outside edges so that the mini book closes properly.

11. Students should choose the main events of the story, write them on each page of the book, and colorfully illustrate them. They can use a ruler to help make neat, even lines of writing. Tell them to use correct spelling and sentence structure.

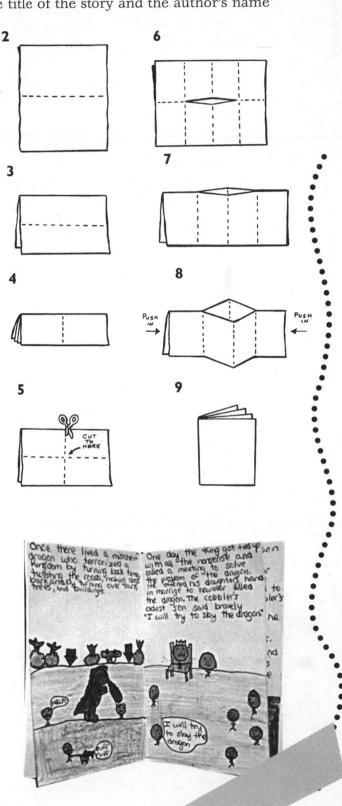

PLOT CARTOON STEP-BY-STEP

1. Divide an 11" x 17" sheet of drawing paper into eight same-size boxes.
2. In the first square, draw a color-fully illustrated cover that includes the title of the story and the author's name.
3. In the second square, list the main characters of the story.
4. Then choose the main events in the plot of the story and draw a cartoon version of the plot in the remaining squares. Students should use a ruler to help make neat, even lines of writing. Tell them to use correct spelling and sentence structure.

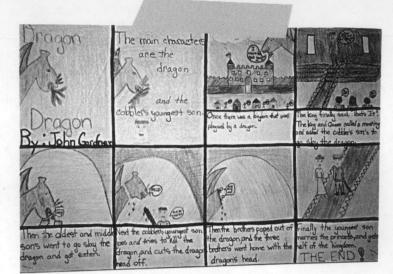

PLOT GRAPHIC ORGANIZER STEP-BY-STEP

1. Using the Plot Diagram reproducible as a model, students present the initiating conflict, rising action, climax, falling action, and resolution on a graphic representation of the story.
2. Tell them to be sure the graphic organizer includes the story title, author's name, student's name, and date.

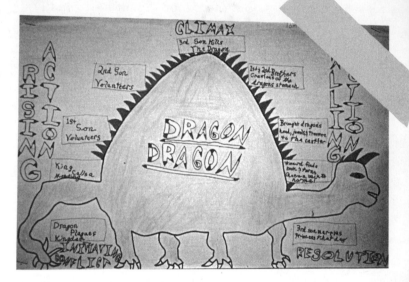

In groups of four, allow students to share the plot projects. Ask them to observe similarities and differences in the projects. Discuss the students' observations and share with the whole class projects that illustrate the differences.

ACTIVITY 3

The Great Plot Race

HOW TO USE THIS ACTIVITY: Use this activity when the class is reading the same short story or novel. It is a great way to help students improve sequencing skills and review the major events in the story.

OBJECTIVE: To sequence the major events of a story

TIME: 15 to 20 minutes

MATERIALS

laminated sets of the major events in the story or novel • manila folders • masking tape • construction paper

STEP-BY-STEP

1. On a computer, prepare a list of the main events in the story or the novel. Using large type (36 or 48 point), type one event per page.

2. Print out the events and laminate them as event cards.

3. Collate the event cards into sets. Mix up the event cards up so that they are not in sequential order. Put each set of events into a folder.

4. Designate sections of the room as "hanging" areas. Students will hang the events in order in these areas.

5. Divide the class into groups of four. Number the group members from 1 to 4.

6. Tell students that they are going to participate in The Great Plot Race. Their intellectual skill and athletic prowess must supersede any Olympic champion's. Explain to students that they will receive a numbered folder. Inside is a set of cards containing the events from the story. At the sound of the signal (for example, a whistle or bell), the group arranges the events in sequential order. As soon as the group has all of the events in order, Runner 1 hangs the first event in that team's area of the room. When Runner 1 returns and *is seated*, Runner 2 hangs the second event. This process continues until all the events are hung. The group that finishes first and has all of the events in proper sequential order wins a prize (for example, candy or a room privilege).

Players are disqualified if:
   - they are too noisy
   - they engage in unsportsmanlike conduct
   - they send a runner before the previous runner is seated
   - their event cards fall down

7. Review the correct order of events with students. Discuss key words that helped them to assemble the events correctly. Answer any questions that arise from this activity.

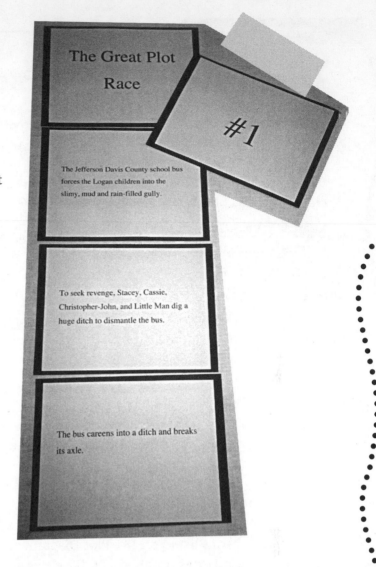

The Great Plot Race

#1

The Jefferson Davis County school bus forces the Logan children into the slimy, mud and rain-filled gully.

To seek revenge, Stacey, Cassie, Christopher-John, and Little Man dig a huge ditch to dismantle the bus.

The bus careens into a ditch and breaks its axle.

TEACHER TIP

This activity actively engages students in learning. Because it is a group activity, students think through the sequencing together and provide reasons why they placed a particular event where they did. Sharing their strategies for sequencing helps students improve their skills.

Life-Size Plot Diagrams

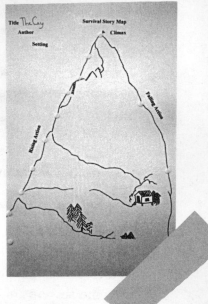

HOW TO USE THIS ACTIVITY: Use this activity to help students summarize self-selected novels at the end of a thematic unit. The activity helps you informally assess students' understanding of the plot. This activity can also be used with short stories or when the class finishes collectively reading a single novel.

OBJECTIVES: To review the concept of plot; to generate a plot map; to summarize a novel

TIME: One 40-minute class period

MATERIALS

Plot Diagram Answer Key for *The Cay*, Plot Diagram Question Sheet for *The Cay*, Plot Diagram Mountain, and Plot Diagram Strips reproducibles (pages 54–57) • Velcro • overhead projector markers • spray bottles filled with water • paper towels

STEP-BY-STEP

1. Distribute Plot Diagram Question Sheet for *The Cay,* or create your own using it as a model. Explain to students that they will use these sheets to create plot diagrams and summaries of the novel.

2. On the photocopy machine, enlarge copies of the Plot Diagram Mountain to poster size. Laminate them.

3. Place Velcro (use the soft side) on the poster-size Plot Diagram Mountain. Use one piece for each event listed on the Plot Diagram Answer Key. Be sure the Velcro is in the appropriate spot. For example, if you have five events in the rising action, place five pieces of evenly spaced Velcro on the rising action section of the plot diagram.

4. Laminate the Plot Diagram Strips. You may need additional sheets if you have more than two events for rising action and two events for falling action.

5. Cut the strips apart and place a piece of Velcro on the back of each one. Since you used the soft side of the Velcro on the map, be sure to use the rough side on the strips.

6. Number group members 1 to 4 and tell them to assume the following group roles:

    1. *Taskmaster:* Keep the group on task and make sure all materials are used properly.
    2. *Organizer:* Assign the questions on the plot diagram question sheet to various group members, making sure that the questions are evenly distributed.
    3. *Gopher:* Gather and return the materials: spray bottle, paper towels, one set of laminated strips, one plot diagram poster.
    4. *Checker:* Use the answer key to check the group's work.

7. Tell the Organizer to divide the questions on the Plot Diagram Question Sheet equally among the group members.

8. Instruct students to write the answers to each question on the corresponding laminated strip. For example, if the student has two "rising action" questions, he or she writes the answers on the "rising action" laminated strips. Answers should be written

in complete sentences with overhead projector markers.

9. Then tell students to place the strips in the appropriate location on the story map.

10. Whoever finishes first fills out the title, author, and setting information.

11. When the group finishes the map, they check it for accuracy. Essentially, they are reading a concise summary of the novel.

12. Distribute the Plot Diagram Answer Key (or one you've created) to the Checker. Laminate it to use as an answer key.

13. To clean up, instruct students to do the following:
    a. Remove the strips from the plot diagram.
    b. Spray one paper towel with water (do *not* spray the laminated strips).
    c. Wipe the strips clean with the wet paper towel and dry them with a dry paper towel.
    d. The Gopher returns all materials.

VARIATION: For more advanced students, eliminate the Plot Diagram Question Sheets. Instead, provide each student with the following trifold.

Have students record the major events at the beginning, middle, and end of the story. Before engaging in the Life-Size Plot Diagrams activity, have students discuss the events on their trifold and identify the initiating conflict, rising action, climax, falling action, and resolution. They may want to color-code the events on their trifold. For example, they can highlight the initiating conflict in yellow, the rising action in pink, etc. Then they can divide the events evenly among group members and write them on laminated plot diagram strips. After completing the activity, students can compare and contrast their diagrams.

Beginning	Middle	End

TEACHER TIP

This is an excellent activity to use as a catalyst for writing a summary.

Categorize a Conflict

HOW TO USE THIS ACTIVITY: Since conflict is a fundamental aspect of plot, teach students about internal and external conflict through categorization and dramatization. Use this activity with novels and short stories. When students are reading different novels, create conflict cards that represent conflicts in the various novels. In this way, students are applying their knowledge of the concept to new material. This activity works best with partners. They take turns categorizing their conflicts and explaining their choices.

INTRODUCTION TO CONFLICT: To introduce conflict, role-play an argument with a student. At the end you both become so angry with each other that you get into a "pretend" fistfight. This really grabs the class's attention. Then tell students that a conflict between two people is called *man vs. man* and is external conflict. External conflicts occur when a character struggles against an outside force. Next, ask students to think of other kinds of conflicts that involve *man vs. something*. Through questioning, try to elicit *man vs. nature* and *man vs. society*.

Have students give examples of *man vs. man, man vs. nature*, and *man vs. society*. Emphasize that *man vs. society* involves a whole group of people, not just one or two.

Then have students think about a time when they had to make a decision. Ask how many of them play mind Ping-Pong by going back and forth weighing different options as they try to make their decisions. Explain that when characters in a novel experience this kind of struggle, it is called *internal conflict*. Like us, the character doubts, wonders, or becomes confused. Have students give examples of internal conflicts that characters face in the novels.

After the discussion, ask students to write the definitions of *external conflict* and *internal conflict* in their notebooks. Beneath each definition, tell them to provide an example of each.

OBJECTIVES: To introduce the concept of conflict; to categorize conflicts from various novels

TIME: 20 minutes

MATERIALS

Conflict Categories reproducible (page 58) copied on white paper (appropriate for *Banner in the Sky, Number the Stars, Hatchet, My Side of the Mountain,* and *The Cay* • Conflict Cards (page 59) copied on pink paper (appropriate for *Banner in the Sky, Number the Stars, Hatchet, My Side of the Mountain,* and *The Cay*) • envelopes • overhead transparency of Categorizing a Conflict Answer Key

STEP-BY-STEP

1. Cut apart the Conflict Cards and Conflict Categories. Put one set of cards into a separate envelope labeled "Categorize a Conflict." Distribute one envelope to each pair of students.

2. Have students spread the white category cards on a desktop. Then put the pink conflict cards facedown in a pile. Ask them to take turns drawing a card and categorizing it. They must decide whether the conflict is *man vs. man, man vs. nature, man vs. society,* or *man vs. himself.* Emphasize that they must explain why they placed the card in a particular category.

3. Use the overhead transparency of the answer key to review the answers as a class. Discuss any questions students have.

TEACHER TIP

As a follow-up activity, I have students dramatize a conflict from a novel. Each group of four students selects two major conflicts in the novel to dramatize. Every person in the group must participate in at least one of the dramatizations. I give the students 5 to 10 minutes to prepare the dramatizations. The class guesses the conflict being portrayed. Then they categorize the conflict.

Plot Diagram Questions for Breaker's Bridge

GROUP MEMBERS' NAMES

DATE _____

_____ , _____ ,

_____ , _____

Answer all questions in complete sentences.

Initiating Conflict #1: What does the emperor demand of Breaker? What will happen if Breaker does not meet the emperor's demand?	**Initiating Conflict:**
Rising Action #2: What does Breaker do to meet the emperor's demand? Is he successful?	**Rising Action:**
Rising Action #2: Whom does Breaker meet, and what does Breaker do for this person?	**Rising Action:**
Climax #3: What does the person give Breaker? What happens to the second one?	**Climax:**
Falling Action #4: Does Breaker successfully build the bridge? What happens to it? What is the emperor's reaction?	**Falling Action:**
Resolution #3: What does the immortal do for Breaker? What is Breaker forced to do for the emperor?	**Resolution:**

Breaker's Bridge Plot Activity Instruction Sheet

GROUP MEMBERS' NAMES   **DATE** _____

_____ , _____ ,

_____ , _____

CONTENT ROLE

1. Initiating Conflict
2. Rising Action

3. Climax and Resolution

4. Falling Action

GROUP ROLE

1. *Gopher:* Retrieve and return materials.
2. *Encourager:* Compliment the group; encourage everyone to work together to get the job finished.
3. *Reporter:* Describe the bridge; share one part of the plot with the class.
4. *Taskmaster:* Keep the group on task; read the group instruction sheet, checking off each item as it is completed.

____ **1.** Share the answers to the Plot Diagram Question Sheet. Check each other for accuracy.

____ **2.** In order of number, take turns reading the passages about the setting and the bridge that you marked with sticky notes. As you listen, visualize what is being described.

____ **3.** Share your sketches of the bridge. Based on the written description in the story, decide which picture is most authentic. Use this one to help you design your bridge.

____ **4.** Send the Gopher for the following items: tape; building materials; 1 white, 2 pink, 1 blue, 1 green, and 1 yellow index card.

____ **5.** Each group member writes the plot information from the Plot Diagram Question Sheet on the appropriately colored index card.
    White = Initiating Conflict   Pink = Rising Action   Yellow = Resolution
    Blue = Climax   Green = Falling Action

____ **6.** The group uses the sketch, text, and building materials to construct the bridge.

____ **7.** Tape the index cards to the bridge. Agree on an appropriate way to have the bridge represent the plot line. Where should the initiating conflict go? Rising action? Climax? Falling action? Resolution? Why?

____ **8.** A Reporter from each group shares one element of the plot with the class. Reporters also briefly describe the bridge and explain how it resembles Breaker's.

____ **9.** Tour the bridges. Which one seems most authentic? Why?

____ **10.** On a sheet of paper, record what the bridge comes to symbolize or represent in the story. Support your statements with evidence from the text. Share and discuss your responses.

Plot Diagram

NAME ______________________ **DATE** __________ **SECTION** __________

____
CLIMAX

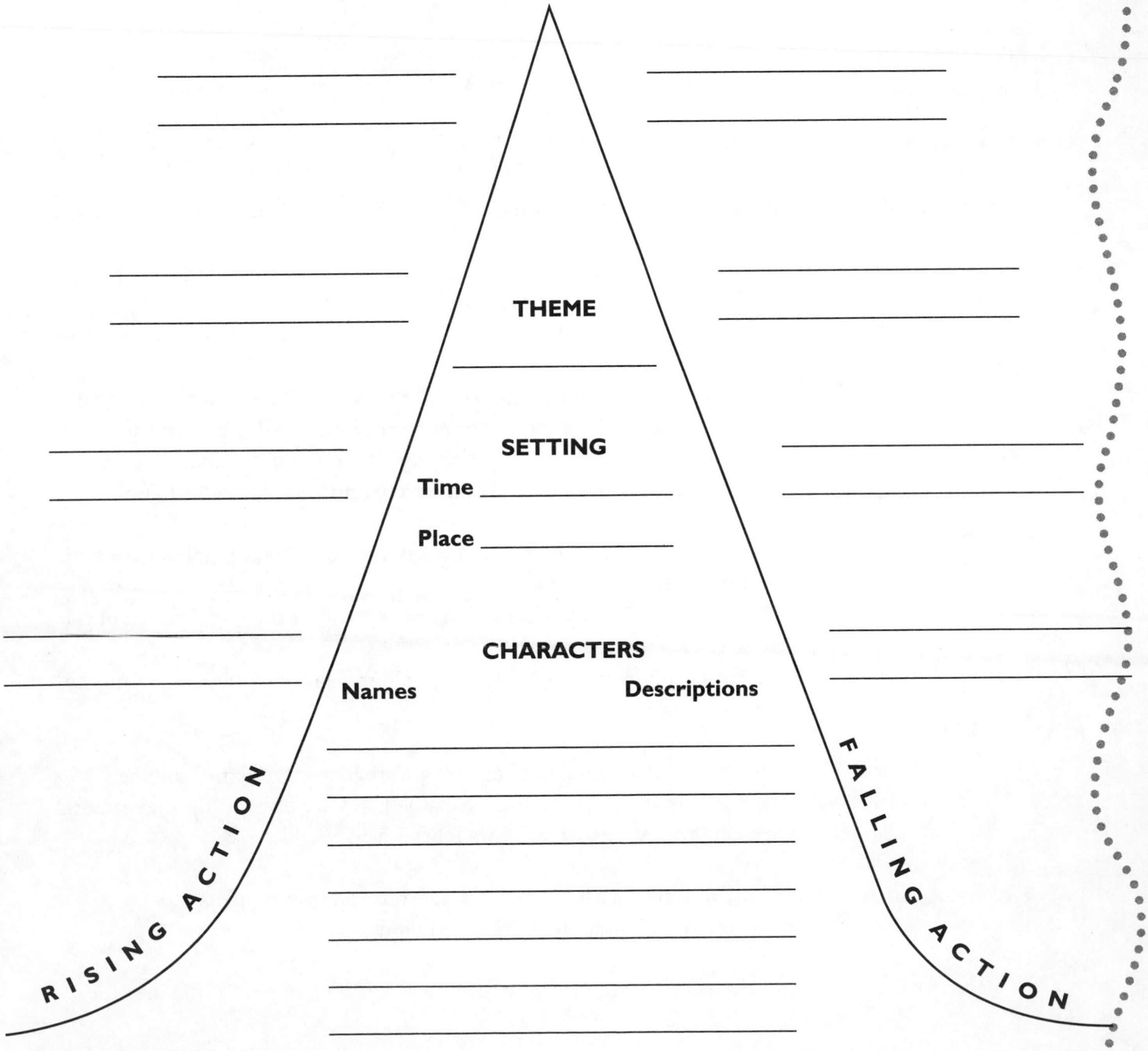
THEME
SETTING
Time ____________
Place ____________
CHARACTERS
Names
Descriptions
RISING ACTION
FALLING ACTION

____
INITIATING CONFLICT

____
RESOLUTION

Plot Diagram Answer Key for The Cay

Title: *The Cay*

Author: Theodore Taylor

Setting: Place: Curaçao, the largest of the Dutch islands off the coast of Venezuela
The cay near Devil's Mouth
Time: February 1942; late summer of the same year

Main Characters: Phillip—prejudiced, selfish, intelligent, resourceful, compassionate
Timothy—protective, fatherly, courageous, knowledgeable, ingenious

Initiating Conflict: The Germans attack the Lago oil refinery on Aruba and blow up six tankers.

Rising Action:
1. While on their way to Virginia, the ship Phillip and his mother are on is torpedoed.
2. Phillip finds himself blind and stranded on a raft in the middle of the ocean with an older black man named Timothy.
3. When Timothy cries that he sees land, Phillip falls overboard into a shark-infested sea.
4. On the island, Timothy constructs a hut of palm fronds, prepares a huge bonfire to signal for help, and uses large rocks to spell "help" in the sand.
5. When Phillip calls Timothy a "stupid, ugly black man," Timothy slaps Phillip, who recognizes he has been wrong and asks Timothy to be his friend.
6. Timothy teaches the blind Phillip how to fish, and Phillip gains the confidence he needs to climb the coconut tree.
7. Timothy protects Phillip when a hurricane ravages the cay, but when the storm is over, Timothy dies.
8. When Phillip plunges into the fishing hole in search of langosta, a moray eel attacks him.

Climax: Phillip hears a plane, lights the bonfire, and realizes the plane can't see white smoke. Later a second plane sees the black smoke Phillip makes with sea grape oil, and American soldiers rescue him.

Falling Action:
1. Phillip is reunited with his parents and returns to Willemstad.
2. After three operations, his sight is restored.

Resolution: Phillip's experience with Timothy on the cay has changed Phillip and the way he views life.

Plot Diagram Question Sheet for <u>The Cay</u>

Use these questions to help you complete the plot diagram.

Initiating Conflict: Who attacks the oil refinery, and what happens?

Rising Action: After Phillip and his mother leave Curaçao, what major conflict occurs?

Rising Action: With whom is Phillip stranded, and what physical problem confronts Phillip?

Rising Action: What important object does Timothy see? After he cries out, what does Phillip do?

Rising Action: What does Timothy construct, and what plan does he develop to signal for help?

Rising Action: Why does Timothy slap Phillip, and how does this experience change Phillip?

Rising Action: What does Timothy teach Phillip to do to acquire food? As Phillip gains confidence, what does he do for Timothy?

Rising Action: What natural disaster occurs, and what are its consequences?

Rising Action: What happens to Phillip as he is searching for langosta?

Climax: How is Phillip rescued?

Falling Action: What happens to Phillip after the American soldiers rescue him?

Falling Action: How many operations does Phillip need, and what physical effect do they have on him?

Resolution: How does Phillip's experience on the cay affect him?

Plot Diagram Mountain

TITLE

AUTHOR

SETTING

CLIMAX

FALLING ACTION

RISING ACTION

INITIATING CONFLICT

RESOLUTION

Plot Diagram Strips

Initiating Conflict
Rising Action
Climax
Falling Action
Falling Action
Resolution

Conflict Categories

# Man *vs.* Man	# Man *vs.* Society
# Man *vs.* Nature	# Man *vs.* Himself

Conflict Cards

The German soldiers close the Jewish shops.	Brian is confused and angry about the divorce.	Brian is angry with his mother and won't speak to her.
Kirsti scolds the two soldiers on the corner.	The porcupine stabs Brian with its quills.	An avalanche tosses Rudi, Winter, Lerner, and Saxo down the mountain.
The Germans attack the American ship *Hato*.	The fire warden searches for Sam because he built a fire during a drought.	Rudi punches the Kurtal bully, Hans Wesselcroft.
Timothy slaps Phillip.	Sam takes the peregrine falcon away from its mother.	The people from Broli dislike and insult the people from Kurtal.
Annemarie wonders why Mama is lying.	Sam feels the need for human companionship.	Phillip feels guilty for mistreating Timothy.

Categorizing a Conflict Answer Key

Man vs. Man

- Brian is angry with his mother and won't speak to her.
- Kirsti scolds the two soldiers on the corner.
- The fire warden searches for Sam because he built a fire during a drought.
- Timothy slaps Phillip.
- Rudi punches the Kurtal bully, Hans Wesselcroft.

Man vs. Nature

- The porcupine stabs Brian with its quills.
- An avalanche tosses Rudi, Winter, Lerner, and Saxo down the mountain.
- Sam takes the peregrine falcon away from its mother.

Man vs. Society

- The German soldiers close the Jewish shops.
- The Germans attack the American ship *Hato*.
- The people from Broli dislike and insult people from Kurtal.

Man vs. Himself

- Brian is confused and angry about the divorce.
- Annemarie wonders why Mama is lying.
- Sam feels the need for human companionship.
- Phillip feels guilty for mistreating Timothy.

CHAPTER 4

Theme

The Purpose of the Theme Activities

At least three of the Standards for the English Language Arts (NCTE and IRA 1996) address the importance of theme. As part of "comprehending, interpreting, evaluating, and appreciating texts," readers must be able to articulate and reflect on the central idea of the story. "To build an understanding of the many dimensions of human experience," students must examine what they learn about the world, people, human nature, and themselves through the text. To respond critically to the text, readers need to be able to connect the author's message to their own lives and to discuss how this message applies to them. If students are "to participate as knowledgeable, reflective, and critical members of a variety of literacy communities," we must actively engage them in activities and discussions related to the heart of literature, the theme.

An Introduction to Theme

Often students confuse plot and theme. For example, when asked to define theme many students respond, "It's what the story is about. 'The Dog of Pompei' was about Mt. Vesuvius erupting." Consequently, it is helpful to do several introductory activities before discussing theme.

Most students have read fables and especially love Arnold Lobel's modern-day versions. After reading, discussing, and interpreting one or two of his fables, give students a list of morals and ask them to write a story that illustrates one moral without stating it. In small groups, have students read their stories, and let the group guess the moral.

To move beyond the moral into theme, photocopy quotations, one for each small group, that reflect the themes of a novel or a story you are reading. Distribute one quote to each group. After reading, discussing, and interpreting the quotation, one member from each group shares the passage with the class and summarizes the group's interpretation. As the interpretations are shared, record each group's theme statement on the board. Then examine characters' actions and events in the story that relate to the various themes. Connect the themes to your own lives and to events and happenings in the real world.

A powerful way to introduce theme involves dramatically reading an inspiring scene or passage and having students respond to it in writing. For example, in the novel *Roll of Thunder, Hear My Cry* by Mildred Taylor, "always meticulously neat, six-year-old Little Man" is outraged when he, a student in all-black Great Faith Elementary School, receives a dirty, damaged, leftover textbook from the all-white school in Spokane County, Mississippi. While reading the inside cover, he discovers that the whites list his race as "nigra." Little Man throws the book on the floor and wildly stamps on it. When he is about to be whipped by his teacher, Miss Daisy Crocker, Cassie, his older sister, defends his behavior:

> "S-see what they called us," [Cassie] said, afraid [the teacher] had not seen.
> "That's what you are," she said coldly. "Now go sit down."

Afterward, Miss Crocker, who is also African American, whips both children. When acting out this emotionally gripping scene, use dialect, gestures, different voices, and simple props to create the characters. Then have students write their response to the scene from Daisy Crocker's, Little Man's, or Cassie's point of view. Students can share their responses with a partner and then discuss their reactions as a class.

Conclude the discussion by defining what the author's message is. Although this incident took place in 1933 before the Civil Rights Act, ask students to think of instances in society today that involve prejudice and injustice. Then talk about ways to combat prejudice. Begin by examining acts of prejudice in your school. Ask students when they have been mistreated and what they can do to prevent it.

ACTIVITY 1

Theme Strips

HOW TO USE THIS ACTIVITY:

Use this simple but effective activity when you are reading different stories or novels; it can be used with any short story or novel.

OBJECTIVES:
To generate a statement about the novel's theme and to relate the theme to your own life; to illustrate the statement with symbols from the novel

TIME:
One 40-minute class period

MATERIALS

sentence strips cut in half (enough for one per student) • colored markers

STEP-BY-STEP

1. Have students write one theme from the story or novel they are reading. Remind them that this should be a general statement about life.

2. With a partner, each student shares the theme statement. Partners check each other for accuracy and clarity, making revisions as necessary.

3. Distribute markers and sentence strips. Ask students to write their theme statements in large, bold print. Have them decorate the borders of the strip to represent the theme.

4. On the back of the strip, students should write several sentences explaining how the theme relates to their lives. Use the example below as a model.

THEME STATEMENT: Turn your fears into imagination. Conquer your fears, and do the impossible.

TEACHER TIP
Use the theme strips as bulletin board borders. Or hang them like a wallpaper border around the walls of your room so students have a chance to read them.

> I love the trampoline, but I am terrified of the diving board. When my friends started teasing me about not going off the board, I decided to try it. After all, bouncing up and down on the end of the board is a lot like jumping on the trampoline.
>
> When I stood at the end of the diving board, I started to shake all over, so I thought about my trampoline and imagined that I was jumping on it. Then I pictured myself as a dolphin diving and plunging through the ocean with my friends. I put my arms up high, ducked my head, and before I knew it, I was in the water. Like Rudi, I conquered my fears and did the impossible. I felt great.

ACTIVITY 2

Theme in a Bottle

HOW TO USE THIS ACTIVITY
Use this activity with novels. It is an excellent way to access students' understanding of theme.

OBJECTIVES: To create a symbol of the theme in the novel; to write a letter from a character's point of view expressing what he or she has learned as a result of his or her experiences

TIME: Three 40-minute class periods or assign as homework

MATERIALS
one bottle per student (large plastic soda bottles work best) • construction paper • scissors • rulers • ribbon • stickers • glitter glue • tissue paper • hot-glue gun (adult use only), rubber cement, or glue sticks • markers, crayons, colored pencils

STEP-BY-STEP
1. Explain to students that a character in the novel wants to express and share what he or she has learned from his or her experiences to help others understand important life lessons. Consequently, the character has decided to send a message in a bottle.

2. Tell students to decorate the bottle with symbols that relate to the main character's message and to the theme of the story. For example, the star on Annemarie Johansen's (the protagonist of *Number the Stars*) bottle represents the Nazis' persecution of the Jews, religious freedom, the courage of the Danes involved in the Resistance movement, and Annemarie's love for her best friend, Ellen Rosen.

3. Explain that students need to write a letter from the main character's point of view. This letter should express the main character's feelings about the life lessons he or she has learned throughout the course of the novel. Use the sample letter below as a model for student writing.

May, 1945

To Whoever Finds This Bottle:

My name is Annemarie Johansen, and I am a twelve-year-old girl who lives in Copenhagen, Denmark. Today the war ended, and the Nazis have been defeated. All over Denmark people are celebrating and bells are ringing. Finally, we are free!

In the last two years I have learned so much. Encountering the Nazi soldiers and their dogs taught me that real courage means facing your fears and moving through them to do what your heart tells you is right and just. Because the Danish people followed their hearts, we saved thousands of lives by hiding and transporting our Jewish friends to safety.

I've also learned how devastating and hideous war is. My heart ripped apart when a Nazi military car ran over my sister Lise. My friends as well as my family suffered grievously. My best friend Ellen Rosen and her parents had to leave their home and country just because they were Jewish. The Nazis were killing the Jews by the thousands, so we had to protect our friends by helping them escape. Then Lise's fiancé Peter, who saved hundreds of Jews' lives, was captured and executed in the public square at Ryvangen. I wept for days and woke up screaming from nightmares in which I relived Peter's and Lise's tragic deaths. I pray for an end to man's inhumanity to man.

But even in the face of the evil and horror that surrounded us, love and goodness prevailed because we acted with justice, compassion, courage, and conviction. Each of us listened to that still, small voice within us that guides us toward the light, and today the light conquered the darkness.

If you find this letter, read it to your friends and family. Pass it from house to house. Let people hear my message and create a world where peace, justice, and human kindness prevail.

Love,
Annemarie Johansen

VARIATION: You can adapt this activity and use it with a small group. Each group member contributes one decoration to the exterior of the bottle, and the group as a whole composes the letter.

TEACHER TIP

After using small bottles, we discovered that large plastic soda bottles work best. Also, wrapping the bottle with construction or wrapping paper eliminates the need for the hot-glue gun.

Theme Song

HOW TO USE THIS ACTIVITY: Have groups and individuals compose and present raps or theme songs to the class. Use this activity with novels.

OBJECTIVES: To compose an original musical score or rap that reflects the theme and mood of the novel; to compose a written paragraph explaining the relationship between the song and the novel

TIME: Two or three 40-minute class periods, or assign as homework

MATERIALS

musical instruments (students bring their own, the music teacher provides some, or students make simple ones, such as percussion instruments)

STEP-BY-STEP

1. Begin by discussing television or movie theme songs with the class. Record and play one or two. If the theme song has lyrics, type and distribute them to students. Discuss the mood and purpose of the theme songs. Ask how they affect us emotionally. The theme song from *Titanic* works well.

2. Explain to students that they will be composing theme songs that reflect the mood and themes of their novels. To assist students in composing a song or rap, encourage them to think of a familiar melody and write their own words to it. Suggest that students make their own simple instruments to use when performing the song in front of the class. The instrument can be as simple as an oatmeal box drum. If students compose an original score, ask them to write a paragraph explaining the relationship between the music and the song. You can use the paragraph below as a model.

My Musical Score for *Banner in the Sky*

   The relationship between the musical composition and the story is that the music, I believe, provides a summary of the story. Although the music I've composed isn't your normal two- or three-sentence paragraph describing the book, it shows what I think some of the main points in the story are. These include *Taps* at the beginning to show Rudi Matt's father's death as he tried to climb the Citadel. The music showing Franz Lerner climbing the Wunderhorn to save Rudi starts out high but then gets low and sad. When Rudi is caught in the avalanche, the music rapidly descends from a high C to a low C. Two high loud Cs and a high B in measures 19 through 21 represent Rudi meeting his father's ghost. In measures 27 and 28, the music takes two leaps up and two leaps down to show Rudi going through the Needle's Eye. Measures 38 through 47 represent Rudi giving up his dream to help the injured Saxo get off of the Citadel alive. There are rests in these measures to show Rudi catching his breath as he struggles.

   The song shows these events from Rudi's point of view and expresses his moods of joy, fear, and sadness. I chose these events because they represent how Rudi changed himself from a boy into a man.

—Patrick Curwen

---

3. Allow students to work individually, with a partner, or in small groups to complete the project.
4. Designate the day students share their songs as "Theme Day." You may want to videotape or tape-record the performances to use as models for next year's class.

ACTIVITY 4

Theme Collage

HOW TO USE THIS ACTIVITY: Use this activity with thematic units and novels.

OBJECTIVES: To create a collage or an illustration depicting the theme of the novel; to verbally explain how the illustration relates to the novel's theme

TIME: Two to three 40-minute class periods, or assign as homework

MATERIALS

magazines • newspapers • scissors • markers, crayons, colored pencils • poster board or large pieces of oak tag • glue sticks

STEP-BY-STEP

1. Explain to students that they are to create a visual representation of their novel's theme. They may create a collage, or an illustration using colors, symbols, images, and patterns to depict the theme.
2. Allow students to work individually, with a partner, or in a small group on the project.
3. Ask students to write a paragraph that explains the meaning of the piece. Use the example on the following page as a model for students.

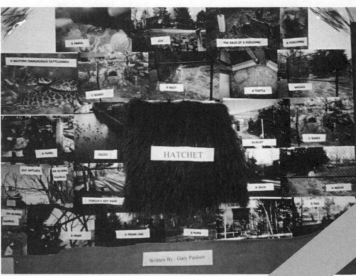

My project relates to the concept of survival because it shows you animals that live in the Canadian wilderness. Seeing the animals here helps you recognize them in the wilderness or wherever you may see them. Besides recognizing the animal, you may be able to tell if the animal is dangerous like the moose was to Brian. Last, you would probably be able to tell which animals would be good for food, like the ruffled grouse (or in Brian's terms "foolbirds"), and which ones weren't good for food.

I learned three things from doing my project. First, I learned some of the animals look mean and vicious, but they're not. Second, I learned some animals, like the bear, won't bother you as long as you don't bother them. Last, I learned that animals and people can live together just like Brian and all the animals that lived in the Canadian wilderness.

—Ashley Bashore

4. Have students share their artwork and their explanations.
5. Create a classroom gallery to display the projects.

ACTIVITY 5

The Theme Tree

HOW TO USE THIS ACTIVITY: Use this activity at the end of a novel unit to assess students' understanding of theme.

OBJECTIVES: To construct an object that serves as a symbol for the theme of the novel; to write a statement of theme

TIME: One 40-minute class period

MATERIALS

construction paper • scissors • glue sticks • rulers • markers • one large sheet of green butcher paper cut into the shape of an evergreen tree

STEP-BY-STEP

1. In small groups, have students state the theme of a novel. Each person in the group must contribute a different statement.
2. Ask the group to make a list of symbols in the novel. Tell them to write what each symbol represents.
3. Have each group member choose a different symbol to construct. On the front, they write the sentence stating the theme. On the back, students write a brief explanation of the object's significance.

4. Have each student share the symbols and theme statement with a partner who is not a member of their group.

5. Glue all of the objects to the theme tree and display the tree.

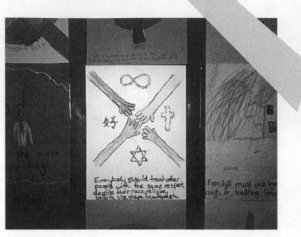

VARIATION: Construct a theme quilt. Cut a class set of 4" x 5 1/2" rectangles. Have students write a statement of theme at the bottom of the square and illustrate it. Glue the squares onto a large piece of rectangular butcher paper. Use colored masking tape to make a border.

CHAPTER 5

Multiple Intelligences Activities for the Literary Elements

The Purpose of the Multiple Intelligences Activities

As Thomas Armstrong (1994) states, Howard Gardner's theory of the multiple intelligences is a "theory of cognitive functioning, and it proposes that each person has capacities in all seven [now eight] intelligences." If "given the appropriate encouragement, enrichment, and instruction," Gardner believes that everyone can develop each of the intelligences to a competent level. Because individuals are unique in the combination of their intelligences, educators must consider "how minds differ from each other" and create curriculum and activities that develop "each student's cognitive profile" (Green 1999). Consequently, "students in today's schools should be given the chance to exercise their intellectual area of expertise." To give students a chance to exercise their "intellectual area of expertise," I ask them to apply their knowledge of the literary elements to a self-selected folk tale and to respond to the story by choosing a multiple intelligences project to complete.

An Introduction to the Multiple Intelligences Activities

During the first month of school, have students complete a multiple intelligences questionnaire, and create activities designed to teach them about multiple intelligences theory. In addition,

TEACHER TIP

I place multiple copies of the directions for each project in separate folders. I label the folders with the name of the project and the intelligence(s) the project addresses. For example, the project "TV Game Show" relates to the linguistic and interpersonal intelligences. Then I spread the folders out on various counters in the room. Students go to the folder of their choice to get the directions they need to complete the project. They may work independently, with a partner, or in a small group. Students store their materials in color-coded pocket folders on which they write their name and section. On a long table in the back of the room, I put out a variety of materials students need to complete their projects. The students are responsible for acquiring the materials I do not provide. After completing the projects, students share them with the class.

incorporate the multiple intelligences into your instruction. Before assigning the multiple intelligences projects related to the literary elements, students should understand what the different intelligences are and what they mean. For these activities to be successful, this knowledge base is essential.

Before students begin the projects, assemble and list eight to ten folk tales on the chalkboard. Give a brief "book talk" about each one and encourage students to peruse the tales before selecting one to read. Since only a few of the tales are rich in flora and fauna, recommend those to students who want to complete the activity related to the naturalist intelligence. Remind students to use the "five-finger method" to determine whether the story is appropriate for their reading level. This simple strategy involves having students select passages from the beginning, middle, and end of the story. Every time students encounter a word they do not know, they hold up a finger. The counting process begins anew on each page. If a student examining a folk tale is holding up four to five fingers per passage, chances are the reading level is too difficult.

After students read the folk tales, describe the multiple intelligences projects and allow them to choose one to complete. One commonality among all of the projects is that they require students to analyze the setting, plot, characters, and theme.

The Multiple Intelligences Projects

OBJECTIVES: To analyze literary elements in a folk tale; to produce a product or performance related to the multiple intelligences

TIME: Five 40-minute class periods, or assign as homework

MATERIALS

8 to 10 folk tales • markers, crayons, colored pencils • craft sticks • oak tag • construction paper • scissors • rulers • glue sticks • tape recorder • blank tapes • CD player • books demonstrating how to make puppets • Folk Tale Multiple Intelligences Project Rubric (page 79)

STEP-BY-STEP

Each set of directions for the activities that follow is designed for the student. You may reproduce them and use them with your class. To evaluate the projects, use the rubric for the Multiple Intelligences Project. You may want to videotape live performances, such as the television shows, puppet shows, and raps. You can use the videotapes as models for next year's students.

Personal Reflections Diary

(Intrapersonal Intelligence)

STEP-BY-STEP

1. Read the folk tale of your choice.
2. Design a cover for your diary. Create an illustration that shows the relationship between you and the story.
3. Inside the cover, on separate sheets of paper, write a reflective piece that includes the following:

    a. Your reaction to the setting. Does it remind you of a place you have visited? Is it so different from what you know that you have difficulty visualizing it?

    b. A character analysis that shows how you are similar to, yet different from, one of the characters.

    c. A description of a conflict in the story. Compare it to a conflict in your life.

    d. A reaction to the culture presented in the folk tale. Describe your attitude toward the culture and discuss similarities and differences.

    e. Pay attention to the moods and feelings the setting, conflict, and plot create for you. Compare them to your own.

    f. Explain how the theme of the folk tale directly relates to your life today.

Design a Travel Brochure

(Linguistic Intelligence)

STEP-BY-STEP

1. Read the folk tale of your choice.
2. Determine the country in which your folk tale is set and design a travel brochure for it. Decide what illustrations you will use and what your format will be. Entice the reader to come to your country.
3. Include a lush description of the setting.
4. Provide an overview of the country's people (the characters in the story).
5. Acquaint the reader with the history of the country. Include information about the major conflict(s), the plot, and the theme here.
6. Describe attractions, lodgings, and restaurants and provide information about transportation and costs.

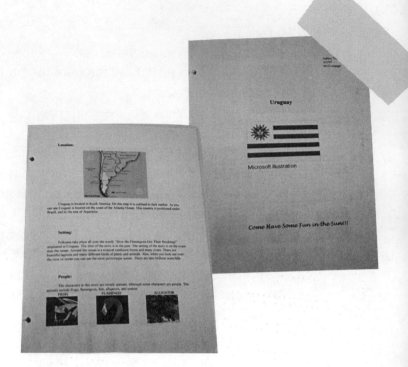

TV Game Show

(Interpersonal and Linguistic Intelligences)

STEP-BY-STEP

1. Read the folk tale of your choice.
2. With a friend, create a television game show that directly relates to your folk tale. Think of current television game shows, such as *Wheel of Fortune,* that you can use as a starting point for designing your game.
3. Provide a clear, detailed description of how to play the game.
4. Design game questions related to the character, setting, plot, and theme of your folk tale. To involve the whole class in the activity, include questions from other stories and novels we have read.
5. Make spinners, pyramids, or anything you need in order to play your game.

Maze

(Logical-Mathematical and Spatial Intelligences)

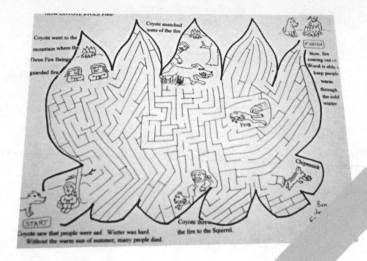

STEP-BY-STEP

1. Read the folk tale of your choice.

2. Decide on the general design that you will use for your maze.

3. Begin the maze with an introduction to the setting, characters, and story problem in your folk tale.

4. Continue the maze by showing events from the story in sequential order.

5. End the maze with the resolution to the story and a reference to the theme.

6. Write a brief paragraph that provides an overview of the folk tale and your maze. Use the following as an example.

> The folk tale *How the Coyote Stole Fire* takes place when man had just stepped onto Earth. A kind, little, brave coyote helped the villagers who were good to Earth and to the animals. The problem is that Coyote overhears the villagers saying that winter is too harsh for their people. Many people die in the winter. To survive, the people need something to keep them warm. Here's a maze for you to try. If you find the right path, you can help the villagers.
>
> —Ben Hess

7. Give the maze to your teacher to make copies for the class.

Graphic Organizer

(Logical-Mathematical Intelligence)

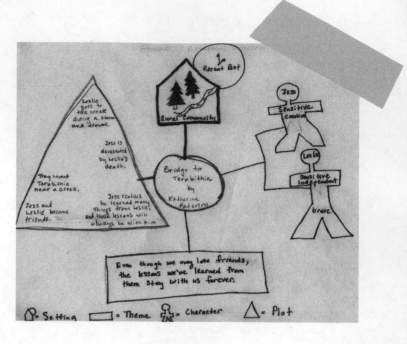

STEP-BY-STEP

1. Read the folk tale of your choice.
2. Decide what patterns, shapes, colors, or images you will use to create your graphic organizer. For example, you might use silhouettes to represent the characters or a map to represent the setting. Be sure to include images for setting, characters, conflict, plot, and theme.
3. Draw the graphic organizer. When it is complete, give it to your teacher to make an overhead transparency for you to use in your presentation. Also, your original will be used to make copies for the class.
4. Provide an answer key for the graphic organizer.

Flora and Fauna

(Naturalist Intelligence)

STEP-BY-STEP

1. Read the folk tale of your choice.
2. Research the setting or environment in which your story takes place. If possible, identify the location's biome. Find passages in the story that describe the setting and use the Internet and library resources to obtain further information about the environment, particularly its plants and animals.
3. Use your research to create a detailed illustration depicting the environment. Include plants and animals. You may use magazines and computer clip art.
4. On a separate sheet of paper, explain how the setting or environment in the story affects the plot, characters, mood, and theme. Use the following example as a guide.

> In the novel *Hatchet* by Gary Paulsen, Brian Robeson, the protagonist, is stranded in the Canadian wilderness. The environment strongly affects the plot and character. For instance, several of the conflicts involve Brian being attacked by an animal. The environment also causes a change in Brian's character. After he encounters a bear and it does not attack him, Brian realizes that he can live in harmony with nature. Before Brian comes to terms with his environment and still fears it, the mood of the story is frantic, and Brian is depressed. When Brian begins to live in harmony with the environment, he becomes hopeful and strong.

Puzzle

(Spatial Intelligence)

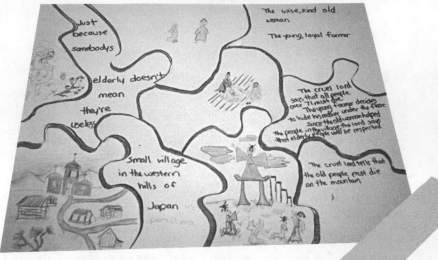

STEP-BY-STEP

1. Read the folk tale of your choice.
2. Design a puzzle on oak tag that illustrates the setting, characters, conflict, plot, and theme of your folk tale. For each element, draw an illustration and write a brief description.
3. Cut the puzzle into pieces so that each illustration and each description is on its own piece.

Game or Sport

(Bodily-Kinesthetic Intelligence)

STEP-BY-STEP

1. Read the folk tale of your choice.
2. Create a game *or* invent a sport that relates to your folk tale. Think of traditional games you might use as a starting point. For example, instead of Capture the Flag you might invent Capture the Character.
3. When designing your game, include ways of incorporating characters, setting, conflict, plot, and theme within it. Also include questions related to stories and novels the whole class has read so that all can participate in the game.

4. Write a set of clear directions that explain how to play the game.
5. Make a list of materials you need to play the game (balls, hoops, spoons). Be sure you provide these materials the day of your presentation.

Rap, Song, or Tape

(Musical Intelligence)

STEP-BY-STEP

1. Read the folk tale of your choice.
2. Decide whether you will write a song or rap in response to the folk tale.
3. Choose a familiar tune or beat.
4. Write the lyrics or verses.
5. Be sure to describe the setting, characters, major conflict, plot, and theme of the folk tale in your rap or song.

OR

STEP-BY-STEP

1. Read the folk tale of your choice.
2. Research the music native to the country in which your story takes place.
3. Make a tape that reflects the mood and theme of your tale. You might want to include recorded music from that culture.
4. Include a written explanation of how this tape reflects the setting, characters, conflict, plot, and theme of your folk tale.

Puppet Show

(Interpersonal and Spatial Intelligences)

STEP-BY-STEP

1. Read the folk tale of your choice.

2. Working in a small group of two or three, make a list of the characters, briefly describe the setting, retell the plot in three to five sentences, and in a single sentence state the theme. Use this as the basis for writing your puppet script.

3. To gather ideas about how to make your puppets, look through books on puppetry. Consider sock puppets, finger puppets, felt puppets to use on a flannel board, wooden spoon puppets, or paper bag puppets. Make a list of the materials the group needs for the puppets. If these items are not in the classroom, you must supply them.

4. Divide these tasks among your group members:
   • Background setting or stage designer
   • Puppet maker 1
   • Puppet maker 2
   • Scriptwriter

5. Produce a puppet show for the class. Include information about the setting, plot, conflict, characters, and theme through your stage design, puppets, and your script. Practice several times before you perform.

Folk Tale Multiple Intelligences Project Rubric

NAME _____ **DATE** _____ **SECTION** _____

Criteria	Outstanding	Good	Acceptable
The project includes a vivid description of the setting and includes both time and place.	4	3	2
The major characters are clearly identified and portrayed.	4	3	2
The major conflict is cited and accurately described.	4	3	2
A detailed, accurate description of the major events is evident.	4	3	2
The theme is clearly stated and captures the heart of the author's message.	4	3	2
The project shows that directions were carefully followed.	4	3	2
The project is creative and original in content and form.	4	3	2
The student(s) presentation of the project was lively, interesting, informative, and clear.	4	3	2

Total Points Possible: 32   **Total Points Earned:** _____

Grading Scale
32–30 = A
29–27 = B
26–24 = C
Below 24 = Not ready yet. Try again.

COMMENTS

Student's Comments: _____

_____

Teacher's Comments: _____

_____

Bibliography

Armstrong, T. 1994. *Multiple Intelligences in the Classroom*. Alexandria, VA: Association for Supervision and Curriculum Development.

Beers, K. , and B.G. Samuels. 1998. *Into Focus: Understanding and Creating Middle School Readers*. Norwood, MA: Christopher-Gordon Publishers.

Caine, G., and R.N. Caine. 1990. "Understanding a Brain-Based Approach to Learning and Teaching." *Educational Leadership* 48(2): 66–70.

Green, F. 1999. "Brain and Learning Research: Implications for Meeting the Needs of Diverse Learners." *Education* 119(4): 682–687.

Jensen, E. 1998. *Teaching with the Brain in Mind*. Alexandria, VA: Association for Supervision and Curriculum Development.

Moore, J. C., W.A. Henk, B.A. Marinak, D. Skiffington, L.M Best, and L.R. Miller, eds. 1989. *The Pennsylvania State Assessment System Tells 1990 Reading Instructional Handbook*. Harrisburg, PA: Pennsylvania Department of Education.

National Council of Teachers of English and International Reading Association. 1996. *Standards for the English Language Arts*. Newark, DE and Urbana, IL.

Nicholson-Nelson, K. 1998. *Developing Students' Multiple Intelligences*. New York: Scholastic Professional Books.

Parnell, D. 1996. "Cerebral Context." *Vocational Education Journal* 71(3): 18–22.

Pennsylvania Department of Education. 1998. *PSSA Classroom Connections: Aligning Standards, Curriculum, Instruction, and Assessment*. Harrisburg, PA.

Routman, R. 1991. *Invitations: Changing as Teachers and Learners K–12*. Portsmouth, NH: Heinemann Educational Books.

Sousa, D. A. 1995. *How the Brain Learns*. Reston, VA: National Association of Secondary Principals.

Tomlinson, C. A. and M.L. Kalebfleisch. 1998. "Teach Me, Teach My Brain: A Call for Differentiated Classrooms." *Educational Leadership* 56(3): 52–55.